Stitching for beginners and beyond

contents

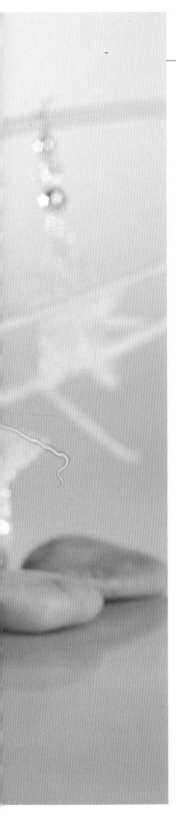

welcome

With so many crafts to choose from why do we choose to stitch? After all isn't embroidery old fashioned, difficult and just not 'cool'? I have loved playing with threads and fabrics for as long as I can remember and to me stitching is so many things, but not these. First of all stitching is fun, relaxing and creative. It doesn't take up a lot of space, is easy to take with you and creates no sticky mess. The materials you use need not be expensive and are readily available.

We all surround ourselves with fabrics, so why not decorate them with threads and beads as people all over the world have been doing it for thousands of years?

The wonderful thing about embroidery is that you can achieve something very unique and decorative knowing just a few basic stitches. The projects in this book each use only a few simple stitches, with some embroidered using just a single stitch. Just look at autumn leaves on page 60 and starburst on page 88.

All the projects on the following pages are easy to make and they have all been rated so you know just how straightforward each is to make. You don't have to be able to sew to create fantastic embroidery. Most of the projects on the following pages are stitched onto finished items so there is no need for machine sewing.

I hope you will look at the projects in this book only as a beginning and add your own creative style and ideas.

Happy stitching,

Anna Scott

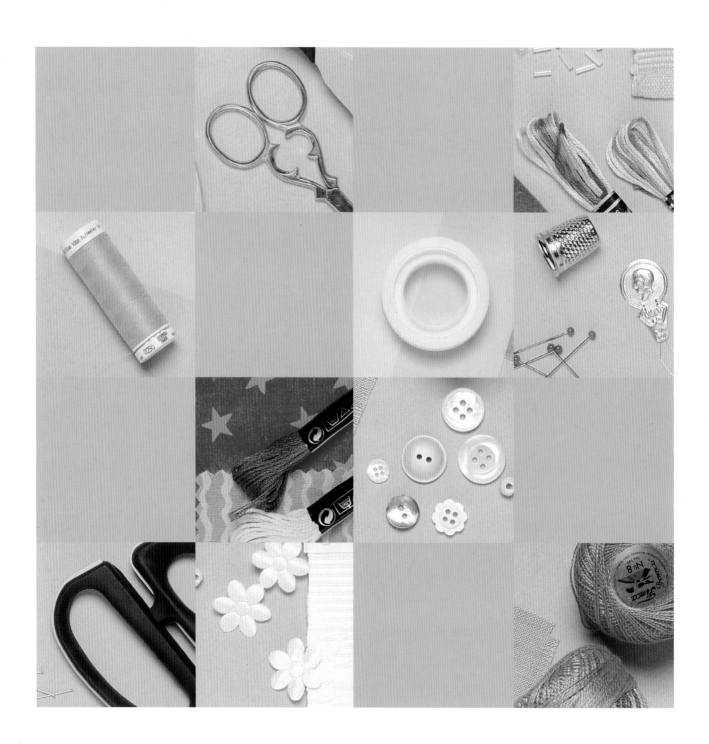

getting started

choosing materials

fabulous fabrics

Almost any fabric can be decorated with embroidery, from fine silk and cotton to cosy wool blanketing, furnishing fabrics and felt. Each project in this book is embroidered on a specified fabric, but you can choose different fabrics to suit your taste.

Your chosen project will influence the type of fabric you use. Likewise the fabric will affect the appearance of the finished item. It is important to keep in mind that in most cases the fabric will show through the stitches. Fabrics with patterns, stripes, checks or woven textures offer background interest that can add extra dimension to your work.

Heavier fabrics are more suited to thicker threads. Lightweight fabrics usually combine well with finer threads but can be stabilised with interfacing if you wish to embroider with thick threads (see page 15). You will also need to stabilise stretch fabrics, such as the top, 'happiness' on page 38.

HOW WILL I KNOW IF THE FABRIC IS RIGHT?

It is always a good idea to work a small sample on a spare piece of fabric to make sure that the fabric, threads and stitches you are about to use will give you the result you are looking for.

Calico

This is a plain, firm, unbleached cotton fabric, excellent for embroidery. Calico can be easily dyed or painted to add extra interest.

Cotton

Cotton fabrics are among the most durable of fabrics. They are available in a large range of colours, patterns and weights, from fine lawns to the heavier poplins and twills.

Felt

This is a very versatile non-woven fabric that will not fray when cut. Traditionally made from wool, today many felts are made from synthetic fibres, so you may need to be very careful if ironing it.

Furnishing fabric

Furnishing fabrics offer some wonderful choices of plain colours or self-patterns, such as damask. You can sometimes obtain small pieces that are suitable for embroidery from upholsterers.

Linen

Linen is strong and durable. It has a natural lustre and the creamy white and neutral fabrics are easily dyed. Linen is available in a variety of weights from fine handkerchief linen to heavy twill.

Silk

Silk is a luxurious and sensuous fabric available in a large variety of colours. It comes in a range of weights and finishes, from fine transparent chiffon and organza to textured silk dupion, heavy twill and brocade.

Wool

Woollen fabrics come in a range of weights and finishes, from fine flannel, ideal for baby wraps, to thick and cosy blanketing.

WHAT IS THE GRAIN OF THE FABRIC?

The grain is the direction in which the threads of a fabric run.

When cutting fabrics, make sure you cut along the grain, following a fabric thread, to ensure you get straight edges.

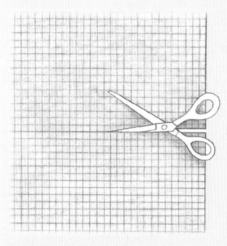

WHAT IS THE BIAS?

The bias of a fabric is diagonally across the grain. If you pull the fabric on the bias you will distort the threads and the shape of the piece. It is particularly important to remember not to pull the fabric on the bias when mounting it into a hoop.

tantalising threads

There is an amazing variety of threads and yarns available for embroidery and choosing can be rather overwhelming.

It is possible to use the very finest of threads right through to lightweight string for stitching. The only real restriction when choosing your threads is that they are suitable for the fabric and type of project you wish to do.

All the projects in this book use stranded cotton or perlé cotton threads. These are some of the easiest and most versatile threads to work with, as well as being readily available.

Stranded cotton

These inexpensive, low sheen threads come in an extensive variety of colours. The threads can be separated into six strands and are very easy to work with. You can vary the appearance of your stitches by altering the number of strands - fewer strands create finer stitches (see hint page 98).

Perlé cotton

This is a lustrous, tightly twisted thread, perfect for creating textured effects. The thread cannot be divided but is available in four different thicknesses - nos. 3, 5, 8 and 12 - the larger the number, the finer the thread.

Variegated and overdyed threads

These are available in stranded cotton, perlé cotton, wool and silk. The gradual change of shade and colour within one skein of thread makes these threads ideal for achieving colour variations.

You can create your own 'variegated' thread by blending strands from different skeins and threading them together in your needle as done for the apples in 'let it snow' on page 56.

Silk threads

A wide variety of silk threads is available, from flat untwisted silks to stranded threads and heavy buttonhole thread. They are prized for their very high sheen, but it takes a little practice to achieve a good result in your stitching.

Some silk threads are not washable because they are not colourfast, so you need to decide whether silk is an appropriate thread for your project.

Wool

Woollen yarns are available in a wide variety of thicknesses and a wonderful array of colours. Fine crewel wool is easy to work with and tapestry wool is perfect for heavier stitching. To prevent the yarn becoming worn as you stitch, use short lengths.

CHOOSING COLOURS

When you buy your threads, always place your selection on a piece of the fabric you intend to use to make sure you get the effect you are looking for. Different coloured backgrounds can alter the appearance of the thread colours.

Study your environment as nature provides many examples of wonderful colour schemes.

Rayon and metallic threads

Rayon threads have a spectacular sheen, loved by many embroiderers. However, they have a mind of their own and can be difficult to use. Use short lengths of thread to minimise twisting and tangling.

Metallic threads can be tricky to work with and often wear easily. Use short lengths to make it more manageable. Make sure you use a needle with a large enough eye to accommodate the thread comfortably.

beads, buttons and braids

There are endless ways to embellish your embroidery. Beads, buttons and braids are just a few and are fabulous for adding texture and sparkle to your projects.

Beads

Beads are available in a multitude of sizes and finishes in all the colours of the rainbow. Small glass beads and bugle beads are those most commonly used for embroidery, but crystals, novelty beads and wooden beads can also be used with great effect.

Sequins

The sparkle of sequins adds amazing glitz to any project. They are available flat or facetted, and most often round, but also come in squares and novelty shapes.

Buttons

Originally used as fasteners in clothing and bed linen, buttons are today used just as much as decoration. There are plenty of novelty buttons available, but ordinary buttons made from wood, plastic or shell can be used very effectively for embellishing embroidery.

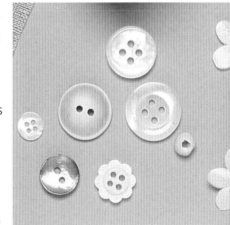

Braids and ribbons

Decorative braids and ribbons are available in an array of widths, colours, patterns and finishes. As well as being used for embellishment, they can be used for borders and to neaten raw edges, while wide ribbons can be used as a fabric, ideal for bookmarks.

Fine silk ribbons can also be threaded into the needle and used for embroidery.

equipment

the basic sewing box

Handstitching and embroidery require only a few very basic tools. Each project on the following pages has a check list of what you need, but it is a good idea to gather some basic equipment for your sewing box before you start.

Needles

Needles come in many types and sizes and it is nice to have a good variety at hand.

The size of a needle is given as a number – the higher the number the finer the needle. Ideally the needle should be of similar thickness to the thread you are using.

The needle chart below gives you an indication of the various types of needles and their uses.

To get started, you could buy a packet of each of the following needles in assorted sizes.

Crewel or embroidery needles are excellent for most types of embroidery. They have a sharp point and a long eye, which makes them easy to thread.

Sharp or sewing needles are good for general sewing. They have a small round eye which minimises wear on the thread. A fine sharp needle is also good for attaching small beads.

Chenille needles are perfect when you stitch with thicker threads, such as tapestry wool, perlé threads or silk ribbons. They are thicker and have a larger eye than crewel needles.

Pins

A box of dressmaker's pins or glass-headed pins, is invaluable for holding tracings or fabrics in place.

OUT OF HARM'S WAY

Try not to leave the needle in your work, as it may rust and leave a mark on the fabric.

NEEDLE	SIZE	SUITABLE FOR
Chenille A thick needle with a large eye. Similar to a tapestry needle but with a sharp tip. This needle was originally used for tufted chenille yarns.	18-24	Suitable for thick threads such as tapestry wool, crewel wool, six strands of stranded cotton, no. 3 and no. 5 perlé cotton, thick silk and heavy metallic thread. Ideal for ribbon embroidery and wool embroidery.
Crewel (Embroidery) A finer needle with a large, long eye. The large eye makes the needle easy to thread.	9-10	Suitable for fine embroidery using one or two strands of cotton, silk or rayon.
	3-8	Excellent general purpose needle. Use with three to six strands of stranded cotton, silk or rayon and fine wool thread, no. 8 and no. 12 perlé cotton and fine metallic thread.
Sharp (Sewing) A good general purpose needle. The small, round eye provides strength for the needle and prevents excess wear on the thread.	10-12	Suitable for fine embroidery. Use with one or two strands of stranded cotton, silk or rayon. The no. 12 is sometimes known as a hand appliqué needle.
	7-9	Use with two or three strands of stranded cotton, silk or rayon.

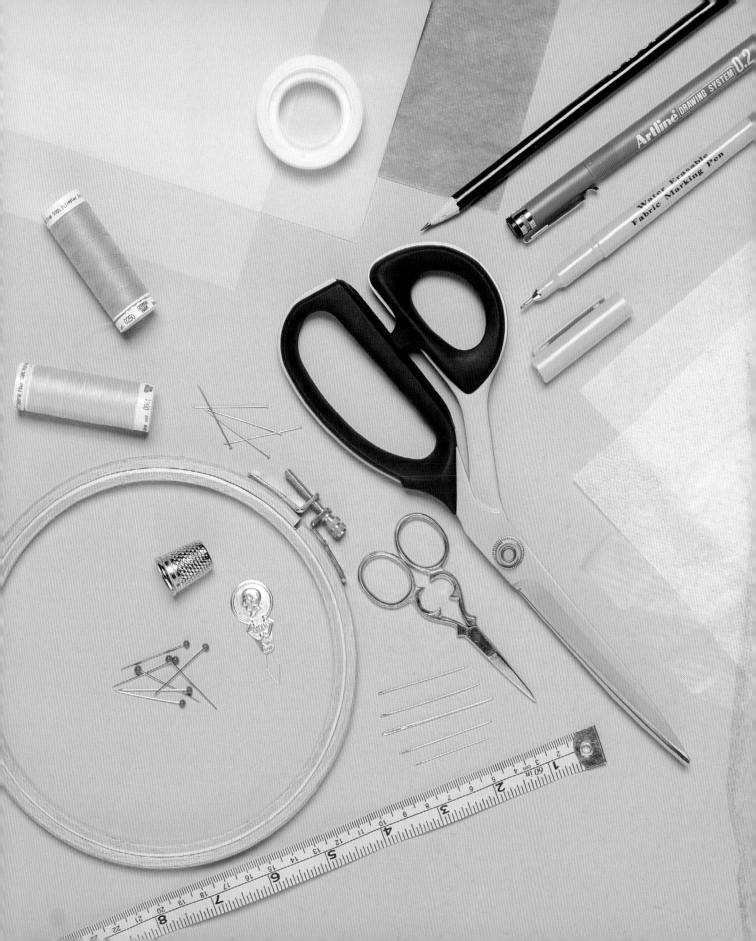

Hoops

Hoops are designed to hold the fabric taut while you stitch and are available in many sizes.

A hoop is made of two wooden or plastic rings. The fabric is placed between the rings and the outer ring is then tightened to hold the fabric firmly in place. When you buy your hoop, look for a good quality one with a firm bracket, that won't bend when the screw is tightened.

Scissors

You will need a pair of small pointed scissors for cutting your threads and a large pair for cutting fabrics.

The most important thing to remember regarding scissors is not to use your embroidery and fabric scissors for anything else! Paper, card and plastic will quickly blunt the blades and ruin your good scissors, so use a separate pair for cutting them.

Needle threader

A needle threader is a small tool with a wire loop designed to make it easier to pass the end of a thread through the eye of a needle.

Thimble

Although not crucial, a thimble can be useful if you do a lot of stitching or are sewing on thick, firm fabrics, such as denim, leather or onto straw, as in the 'spring time' bag on page 84.

Place the thimble over your middle finger and use it when pushing the needle through the fabric.

Tacking thread

Machine sewing thread is used for tacking. Use light colours to avoid leaving permanent marks in the fabric (see page 16).

tools for transferring

There are many ways to transfer a design onto fabric. It is good to have a small collection of tools on hand for this purpose.

Pens

Fine permanent pen, black or dark brown, is useful for tracing the design onto paper or water-soluble stabiliser.

Sharp lead pencil or mechanical pencil, is used for tracing directly onto the fabric. The lines will disappear in the wash, but it is best used when the lines will be covered completely by stitching. You can also use a very sharp coloured pencil in a shade close to those of your threads.

Fine water-soluble fabric marker is used for tracing directly onto fabric. The pen is ideal if the stitches will not be covering the design lines completely, because the marks will disappear when the fabric is sponged or rinsed with cold water. It is important to remember not to press the fabric before rinsing as heat will make the pen permanent.

Paper

Tracing paper is essential for tracing the embroidery design from the pattern sheet. You can also use baking paper for this purpose.

Dressmaker's carbon paper comes in several colours. It is great for thick and dark coloured fabrics with a smooth surface.

, is a very
de. The
liqué paper
n dry out

lising with

ailable in
ome are
e. Choose
ic you wish
be able to

ter-soluble
d. Store your

ing fabrics.
s.

ape

titching
straight lines see 'all that glitters' page 32.

ready, set, stitch

With embroidery, as with most other things, you will achieve a better result if you take the time to prepare carefully.

how to prepare the fabric

Washing

Many fabrics will shrink a little when they are washed for the first time. Dark or bright colours will often contain some excess dye, which will come out in the first wash. It is therefore a good idea to wash fabrics before you begin your stitching to avoid any nasty surprises later. Wash your fabric or garment following the manufacturer's care instructions.

Raw edges

When you handle a cut piece of fabric, the edges will loosen and begin to fray. To prevent this happening, neaten the raw edges with a machine zigzag or overlock stitch, or by hand with an overcast stitch.

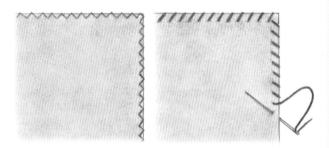

Alternatively, fold each side of the fabric twice to enclose the raw edge and tack in place.

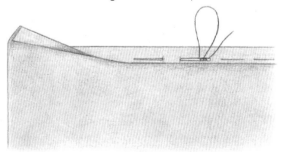

Tacking

Tacking is a row of temporary stitches used to hold pieces of fabric together, or to mark out placement guides for positioning your embroidery design. Tacking is best worked using a light coloured machine sewing thread.

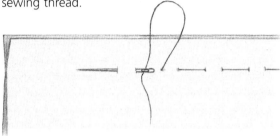

how to prepare the threads

There are a few simple steps to follow to prepare your threads for use.

Colourfastness

Make sure the threads you are about to use are colourfast. Many threads will have this information on the tag, but it is a good idea to test the thread if you are unsure.

- Cut off a short length of thread and wet it.
- Place the thread on a piece of paper towel or tissue and press between your hands.
- If the colour bleeds into the paper, the thread is not colourfast.

Looped skeins

Most stranded threads, and some woollen yarns, come as looped skeins.

- Leave the tags on the skein. Some skeins have a little paper lock on one tag which you need to remove. Gently pull out the end of the thread from the centre of the skein.
- Alternatively, remove the tags and wind the thread onto a card.

Twisted skeins

Nos. 3, 5 and 8 perlé threads and some silks and wools are sold as twisted skeins.

- Slide the tags off the skein and keep the one with the thread number. Untwist and open the skein and cut all the threads at one end. Fold the bundle in half and slide the numbered tag back onto the threads.

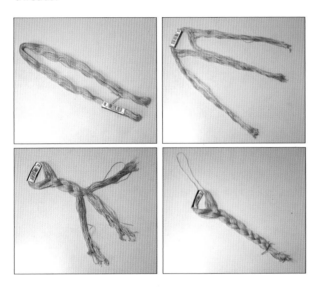

- Divide the threads into three even groups.
- Plait the threads loosely.
- Tie the ends with another piece of thread. To remove a strand, simply pull gently from the tag end.

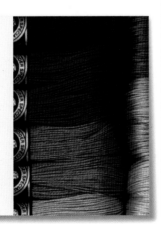

HOW LONG IS A LENGTH OF THREAD?
It is best to work with threads no more than 35cm (14") in length, or the distance from your thumb to your elbow. Longer threads will wear and easily become tangled.

Separating strands - stripping

When you need to use more than one strand at a time, it is important to separate the strands and then put them back together. This is known as 'stripping' the thread.

- Hold the end of all six strands between your thumb and index finger.
- Ease out a single strand and pull it upwards, out of the bundle. Do not 'peel' it off.

- The remaining strands will fall back neatly.
- Repeat for the number of strands you need before re-grouping them and threading them into the needle.

UN-DO THE TWIST

Threads can often twist as you work. To untwist the threads, let the needle hang freely at regular intervals. The thread will spin back to the correct amount of twist.

tricks to threading needles

Getting the thread into the eye of a needle need not be a daunting task.

- Make sure you have cut the end of the thread cleanly. If you have any stray fibres sticking out of the thread end, they can push the thread away from the needle when you try to thread it.
- The eye in most needles is elongated, so to make the thread fit the eye, flatten the end between your fingers.
- You can moisten the thread by licking your fingers and running the end of the thread between them. Trim away the moist piece after threading.

Needle threader

- Bring the wire loop of the needle threader through the eye of the needle.
- Slip the thread through the wire loop.
- Pull the threader back out of the needle eye, drawing the thread with it.

Loop method

Another method is to fold the thread around the needle.

- Pinch tightly around the needle and thread.
- Pull the needle upwards and out. The folded thread will sit between your thumb and index finger.

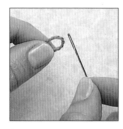 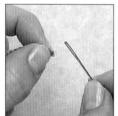

 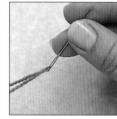

- Push the eye end of the needle between your fingers, slipping the eye of the needle onto the folded thread.

HAVING TROUBLE?

The eye of a needle has a right and a wrong side. Try turning the needle and threading it from the other side.

If you are having real trouble, try a larger needle.

---

positioning designs

Most of the designs in the liftout pattern sheet have placement guides to assist you when positioning the design onto fabric.

The instructions for each project will explain how to prepare your fabric or item to position the design correctly.

transferring designs

Some of the easiest transfer methods are used for the designs in this book. Which method to use depends on the fabric and the nature of the design. Each project on the following pages includes instructions for the transfer method appropriate for the materials used.

Direct tracing

This method is suitable for light coloured fabrics.

- Place a piece of tracing paper over the design and hold it in place with paper clips or removable tape.
- Use a fine permanent pen to trace the design onto the tracing paper.
- Tape the tracing to a window or light box. This step can be omitted for sheer fabrics.
- Position the fabric over the tracing with the right side facing up. The light shining through will make the design visible through the fabric.
- Use a sharp lead pencil or water-soluble fabric marker to trace the design onto the fabric.

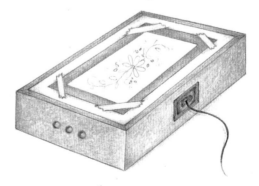

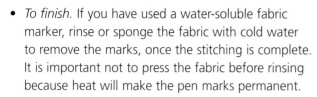

- *To finish.* If you have used a water-soluble fabric marker, rinse or sponge the fabric with cold water to remove the marks, once the stitching is complete. It is important not to press the fabric before rinsing because heat will make the pen marks permanent.

Dressmaker's carbon paper

This is the easiest way to transfer onto thick and dark fabrics with a smooth surface, such as cotton, silk and linen. Use a paper colour that blends with the colour of your threads as the lines can be permanent.

- Place a piece of tracing paper over the design and hold it in place with paper clips or removable tape.

- Use a fine permanent pen to trace the design onto the tracing paper.

- Position the traced design over the fabric and pin it in place at the two upper corners.

GENTLY DOES IT

Try not to rub your hands over the paper while you trace to avoid making smudge marks on the fabric.

- With the coloured side facing the fabric, slide the carbon paper between the fabric and the tracing.

- Trace over the design lines with a firm, even pressure, using a pencil or ball point pen.

- Carefully lift one corner of the tracing and carbon paper to make sure all the lines have been transferred before you remove the pins.

Templates

This is a fantastic way to transfer simple shapes that are repeated several times.

- Draw or trace the shape onto tracing paper with a fine pen.

- Turn the paper over and retrace the shape with a lead pencil.

- Place the tracing, with the pen side facing up, over a piece of lightweight card and hold it in place with tape or paper clips.

- Trace over the shape again, with a firm even pressure, using a pencil or ball point pen. The lines will transfer onto the card.

- Remove the tracing and cut out the shape from the card, just inside the traced lines.

- Position the card template onto the fabric and hold it in place while you draw around it with a sharp lead pencil or water-soluble fabric marker.

LOOK AROUND YOU

Everyday items such as drinking glasses, plates and coins make excellent templates for circles.

Water-soluble stabiliser (Solvy)

This amazing material is particularly useful for coarse fabrics and fabrics which are difficult to trace onto, such as knitted and textured fabrics like the tea towels in 'paper dolls' on page 30.

It is recommended that you use a hoop when using this method.

- Place the Solvy over the design and hold it in place with paper clips or removable tape.

- Use a fine permanent pen to transfer the design lines directly onto the Solvy.
- Position the Solvy onto the fabric and tack it in place around and across the design.
- Place the fabric in the hoop (see opposite page).
- Stitch the design through both layers.

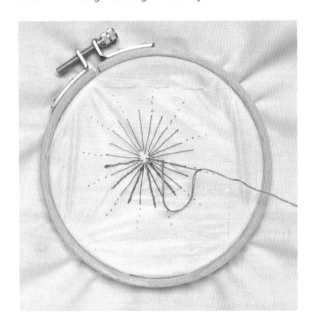

- *To finish.* Once the embroidery is complete, remove the hoop and tacking threads. Trim the Solvy close to the edges of the embroidery.
- Rinse or sponge the embroidery in cold water and watch as the Solvy disappears before your eyes.

WITHOUT A TRACE

Take care when transferring a design with pencils, marking pens or dressmaker's carbon. Some marks can be permanent or difficult to remove and you will need to cover them with embroidery.

If you are unsure, test on a small scrap of fabric before you begin.

using a hoop

Whether or not to use a hoop is very much a personal choice. Though not essential, you will often get a better result when using a hoop, especially when you stitch on lightweight fabrics.

Choose a hoop large enough for the design to fit inside the ring, so you avoid flattening finished sections of embroidery.

Binding a hoop

Binding the inner ring of the hoop will prevent the fabric from slipping while you stitch. To bind it you can use white cotton tape or bias binding ironed flat.

 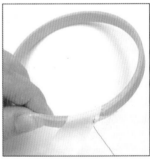

1. Hold the end of the binding and wrap it around the inner ring of the hoop.

2. Secure the binding with small back stitches at the edge of the binding.

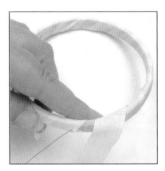 

3. Wrap the binding around the hoop, ensuring there are no creases and the layers of binding overlap.

4. When reaching the starting point, cut off the excess binding and secure the end with small back stitches.

Placing fabric in a hoop

- Loosen the tension screw so the two rings slip apart.
- Place the inner ring on a table and position the fabric over the ring.
- Press the outer ring down over the fabric and tighten the screw.

- If you need to tighten the fabric further, make sure you pull only with the grain of the fabric. If you pull the fabric on the bias it will stretch and become distorted (see page 10).
- Take the fabric out of the hoop when you are not stitching, to avoid leaving a permanent mark.

TO SEW OR NOT TO SEW

Most stitches can be either 'sewn' or 'stabbed'. Always stab the needle through the fabric when working in a hoop, as skimming the needle will distort the fabric.

sewn   stabbed

good beginnings ~ happy endings

Securing your threads

It is important to secure the thread when you start and finish, so that your stitches don't come undone.

When you stitch on articles that require regular washing, such as clothing, you need to take extra care because washing can loosen the threads. There are a number of ways to begin and end a thread – the most important thing is to try and avoid unsightly lumps and large knots on the back of your work.

Stitching

This method is quite secure and is suitable for almost any type of embroidery.

- Begin in an area that will be covered by embroidery and close to the starting point for the stitching. Leave a short tail and take two tiny stitches on the back of the fabric, splitting the first stitch.

- Work a few more stitches into the first two to secure the thread firmly. Trim the tail.
- Finish in a similar way, with several small back stitches into the stitches on the wrong side of the fabric. Make sure the thread doesn't show on the front.

Weaving

Weaving is suitable only for stitching that will not need washing as the thread tails can come undone.

- Begin by leaving a 10cm (4") tail of thread hanging on the back of the fabric.
- After working a small part of the embroidery, re-thread the tail and weave it under the stitches on the back. For added strength, make two or more small stitches into the back of the work. Trim the thread tail.
- Finish in the same way.

Knots

These are easy to use when you have a textured surface, such as thick embroidery, beads and buttons, so the small lump from the knot won't show on the front.

A knot combined with a back stitch is very secure and ideal for embroidered clothing and table linen.

- Thread the needle. Hold a short tail of thread along the shaft of the needle with the tail towards the eye.
- Hold the tail and the needle in one hand. With the other hand, wrap the thread around the point of the needle 2 - 4 times.
- Holding the wraps between your thumb and index finger, pull the needle through the wraps. This creates a neat, consistent knot.

- Finish as for stitching (see page 21).

finishing your work

Cleaning and pressing

Once the stitching is complete the project will need to be 'finished'. This may involve washing, or if the fabric or threads are not colourfast or washable, you may need to visit the dry cleaner.

Wash the work by hand in lukewarm water using a mild detergent, or on a gentle machine cycle with the embroidery placed inside a pillowslip.

- Be careful not to rub the surface of your stitching as that will cause pilling.
- Rinse the work thoroughly in clean water.
- Roll it up in a clean towel and press as much excess water out as possible, but do not wring it.
- Dry the piece flat, as quickly as possible, away from direct sunlight.

Pressing your embroidery can make a huge difference to the overall finish of the work. Avoid pressing the right side as this will flatten the threads too much.

- Fold a towel into a few thicknesses and place it on your ironing board.
- Place the work, with the embroidery facing down, onto the towel and press the back of the work using a setting appropriate for the fabric. The stitches will sink into the towel and you will be able to press the fabric flat.

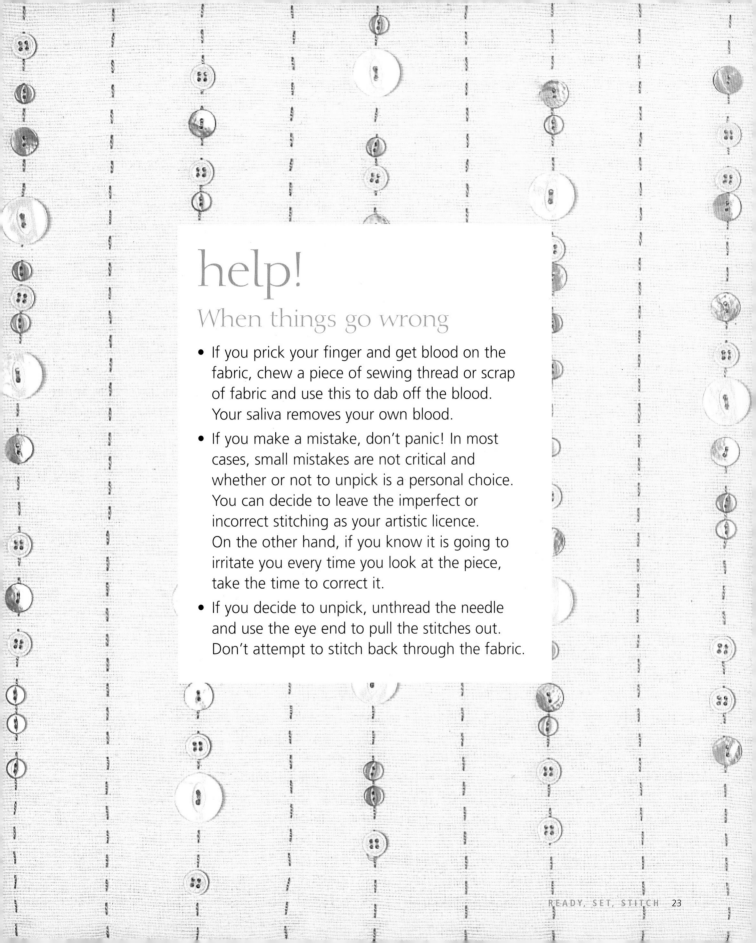

help!

When things go wrong

- If you prick your finger and get blood on the fabric, chew a piece of sewing thread or scrap of fabric and use this to dab off the blood. Your saliva removes your own blood.

- If you make a mistake, don't panic! In most cases, small mistakes are not critical and whether or not to unpick is a personal choice. You can decide to leave the imperfect or incorrect stitching as your artistic licence. On the other hand, if you know it is going to irritate you every time you look at the piece, take the time to correct it.

- If you decide to unpick, unthread the needle and use the eye end to pull the stitches out. Don't attempt to stitch back through the fabric.

project gallery

sunshine

 VERY EASY

YOU WILL NEED

FABRIC
> Cotton fabrics for appliqué
  Blue
  Orange
  Red
  White
  Yellow

SUPPLIES
> Jeans
> White buttons
> Blue buttons
> Orange button

THREADS
> Stranded cotton
  Blue
  Orange
  Red
  White
  Yellow

EQUIPMENT
> Appliqué paper
> Water-soluble fabric marker
> Sharp pencil
> No. 8 sharp needle

Getting started

See the liftout pattern sheet for the appliqué templates.

Preparing the fabrics

Trace the appliqué templates onto pieces of appliqué paper.

- Trace the large and medium flowers twice and the small flower once. Trace two large circles, three medium circles and two small circles.

- Cut the flower templates out and fuse them to the back of the fabrics (see step 2, page 114).

Diag 1

- Cut out each flower shape 3mm (1/8") from the edge of the paper *(diag 1)*.

- Prepare the circles following steps 1 - 5 on page 113.

- Fuse a medium flower to each large flower, offsetting the position of the petals *(diag 2)*. Fuse a large circle in place at the centre of each flower.

- Arrange the flowers and circles on the jeans and fuse them in place.

Diag 2

CUTTING APPLIQUÉ SHAPES

Whenever you cut though appliqué paper, we recommend that you don't use your fabric or embroidery scissors because the paper backing will blunt the blades.

How to stitch the design

Work the French knots with three strands of cotton and all other stitching with two strands. Strip the threads and keep them untwisted while you work (see page 17).

Order of work

Large flowers

- Stitch a row of running stitch around the edge of the outer petal, 3mm (1/8") from the edge *(diag 3)*. Stitch a second row just inside the first.

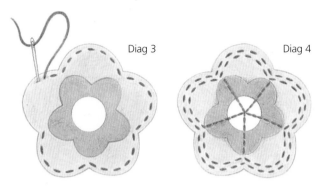

Diag 3   Diag 4

- Beginning each at the centre, work back stitch lines through all layers to the tip of each inner petal *(diag 4)*.

- Stitch rows of back stitch between the previous rows, finishing each with a stitch over the edge. Add two stitches in a V shape *(diag 5)*.

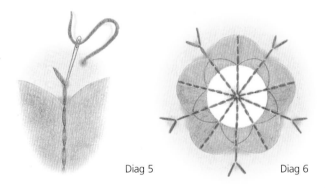

Diag 5   Diag 6

- Using the water-soluble fabric marker, draw five petals around the centre circle *(diag 6)*. Embroider the petals with back stitch

Small flower

- Stitch a single row of running stitch around the flower 3mm (1/8") from the edge.

- Work rows of back stitch from the centre and over the outer edge to define the petals. Finish each row with two stitches in a V shape as you did on the large flowers.

Circles

The circles are edged with blanket stitch, worked with the 'legs' of the stitches facing out like rays.

- Bring the needle to the front 3mm (1/8") inside the edge of the circle. Take a stitch under the edge of the circle *(diag 7)*. Pull the thread through for the first stitch. Continue to work blanket stitch evenly around the circle.

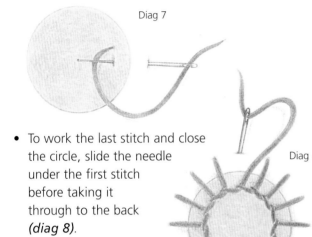

Diag 7

- To work the last stitch and close the circle, slide the needle under the first stitch before taking it through to the back *(diag 8)*.

Diag 8

- Using three strands of thread, work a French knot at the end of each ray.

Button centres

Stitch a button in place at the centre of each flower and circle using a contrasting thread (see page 111).

WASH BEFORE YOU STITCH

New garments, especially dark colours and red, will often contain excess dye. To avoid ruining your stitching in the wash, always wash new garments before you begin your project.

IMAGINE THIS

These easy appliqué flowers would look equally fantastic on a cushion or tote bag - and if you are not keen on strong colours, try using some soft pastels for a more delicate look.

SUPPLIES

> White tea towel
> Red tea towel
> 12cm x 50cm wide
  (4 ³/₄" x 20") piece of
  water-soluble stabiliser
  eg Solvy for each design

THREADS

> No. 8 variegated perlé
  cotton
  Navy
  Red

EQUIPMENT

> Fine permanent pen
> No. 4 crewel needle

paper dolls

stitches used

back stitch, page 115

 **SUPER EASY**

Getting started

See the liftout pattern sheet for the embroidery designs.

Test to see that your tea towels and threads are colour fast (see page 16).

Transferring the design

Trace one design onto the stabiliser paper (see page 19). Position the tracing over one end of a tea towel, parallel to the edge. Tack the tracing in place along each side and at regular intervals across the design to prevent it from slipping while you stitch *(diag 1)*.

Diag 1

How to stitch the paper dolls

- Secure the thread on the back at one side of the tea towel (see page 22).
- Work back stitch along the design line. Keep the stitches short to achieve nice round curves.
- To begin a new length of thread, choose a section of thread that is close to the colour of the last stitch *(diag 2)*.

Diag 2

Finishing

Trim and dissolve the stabiliser (see page 20).

YOU CAN ALSO TRY...

The paper dolls would also look great around the hem of a little girl's denim or corduroy skirt or along the edge of a bath towel. If you are stitching on a towel, you should use a no. 5 perlé thread so the stitching doesn't disappear into the pile of the towelling.

The blue paper doll border measures 8.5cm (3 3/8") in height.
The red paper doll border measures 7.5cm (3") in height.

The front of this book cover measures 23cm x 15cm wide (9" x 6").

buttoned up

YOU WILL NEED

FABRIC
> Red felt
> Yellow felt

SUPPLIES
> Notebook
> Five assorted buttons

THREADS
> Stranded cotton
   Christmas red
   Dark navy blue
   Dark royal blue
   Orange
   White
   Yellow

EQUIPMENT
> Ruler
> Lightweight card
> Magic tape
> No. 4 and no. 8
   crewel needle

☺☺☺ **SUPER EASY**

Getting started

How to work out the size for your book cover

- Measure the notebook from front edge to front edge, around the spine, using a tape measure *(diag 1)*. Add 15cm (6") to this measurement for the flaps to go around the front edges of the book. This measurement is the width of the felt (A).

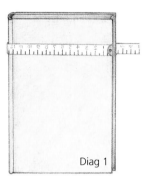

Diag 1

  Measure the length of the book and add 1.5cm (5/8") to your measurement for the seam allowance. This measurement is the length of your cover (B).

- On the red felt, rule lines at these measurements *(diag 2)*. Cut out just inside the ruled lines.

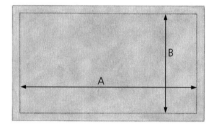

Diag 2

Bookmark

Use the ruler and pen to mark a 2.5cm (1") wide piece on the yellow felt. Cut the strip 4cm (1 1/2") longer than the book cover.

Transferring the design

- Using the ruler, measure 7.5cm (3") in from each side of the red felt and mark with pins. Place a length of magic tape along the outside of each row of pins *(diag 3)*.

7.5cm   7.5cm

Diag 3

- Fold the piece of felt in half along the length and place pins and tape along the foldline to mark the spine. Unfold the felt. Remove the pins.

- Use a selection of coins as templates for the buttons (see page 19). Arrange the coins randomly over the right hand section of the cover, between the rows of tape. Trace around each with the pen.

- If two button shapes overlap, remember to trace the full circle for only one button *(diag 4)*.

- You don't need to mark the 'holes' as these are easy to place as you stitch.

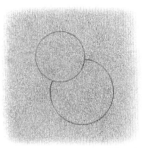

Diag 4

How to stitch the design

All embroidery is stitched with three strands of cotton in the small needle. Strip the threads and keep them untwisted while you work (see page 17).

Book cover

Order of work

- Work the outline of each button in back stitch. Keep the stitches relatively short to achieve nice round curves *(diag 5)*.

Diag 5

- Stitch two or four French knots at the centre of each circle for the holes in the buttons. Use the same colour thread for the holes as you used for the outline.

- Using the yellow thread, work a row of running stitch along the inside edge of the tape at each marked foldline for the flaps *(diag 6)*. Remove the tape.

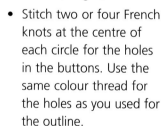

Diag 6

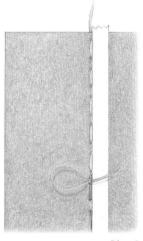

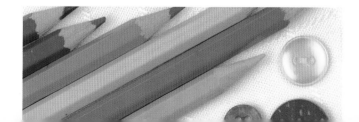

How to make the cover

- To make the flaps, fold each end of the felt to the inside along the row of running stitch and pin in place *(diag 7)*.

  Secure the yellow thread between the layers of felt. Stitch along each side of the cover in running stitch to secure the flaps, using a 6mm (¼") seam allowance *(diag 8)*.

Diag 7

Diag 8

- Slip the front and back edge of the notebook into the flaps to cover the book.

How to make the bookmark

- Work a row of running stitch along each side of the yellow felt, using red thread on one side and blue on the other.

- Stitch a button in place at each end (see page 111).

- Thread the large needle with two strands of both red and blue thread. Take the needle through the holes of a new button twice, positioning the button halfway along the threads *(diag 9)*.

Diag 9 - back of button

Bring the threads together and thread all eight ends into the needle. Take the threads through both holes of two more buttons to make a button tassel *(diag 10)*. Secure the threads behind the button at one end of the bookmark.

Diag 10 - back of buttons

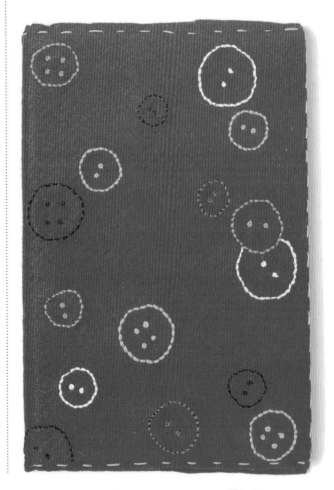

tall ships

stitch used

blanket stitch, page 118

technique used

appliqué, page 113

 **SUPER EASY**

YOU WILL NEED

FABRICS
> Cotton fabrics to complement your towel

SUPPLIES
> Towel
> Face washer

THREADS
> Stranded cotton
Colours to match your fabrics
> No. 5 perlé cotton
White

EQUIPMENT
> Appliqué paper
> Sharp lead pencil
> No. 4 and no. 8 crewel needles

The sailing boat measures 7.5cm x 8cm wide (3" x 3 1/8").

Getting started

See the liftout pattern sheet for the appliqué templates.

If you are using strong colours like the towels shown, wash them before you begin to make sure any excess dye can't ruin your work later.

Preparing the appliqué pieces

- Trace each template onto appliqué paper and repeat for as many sailing boats as you are planning to stitch.

- Prepare and fuse the pieces in place following the instructions on page 113 and referring to the photograph for placement.

How to stitch the boats

The appliqué pieces are outlined in blanket stitch, using two strands of matching stranded cotton in the small needle. Remember to strip the threads and keep them untwisted while you stitch (see page 17). Use the larger needle when you are stitching with the perlé thread.

Order of work

Sailing boat

- Bring the thread to the front just beyond the edge of the appliqué fabric, at one corner of a shape, and work blanket stitch along the edge.

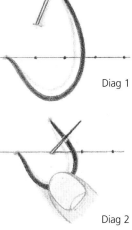

Diag 1

Diag 2

Because the towelling is so thick, you will get the best result by stabbing, rather than skimming the needle through the fabric *(diags 1 & 2)*.

- To turn the corners, work three stitches into the same hole in the fabric *(diag 3)*.

Diag 3

Waves

- Stitch a row of large blanket stitch along the edge of the woven band on the face washer, using a doubled length of white perlé thread in the large needle.

- Work the waves on the towel in a similar way, gradually changing the height of the stitches to form the larger waves *(diag 4)*.

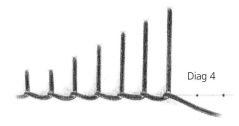

Diag 4

IMAGINE . . .

how great these ships would look on a little boy's blanket or bed sheets - or in the corner of a set of placemats.

happiness

YOU WILL NEED

SUPPLIES
> Royal blue knitted top
> 20cm x 15cm wide (8" x 6")
  piece of lightweight fusible
  interfacing
> 20cm x 15cm wide (8" x 6")
  piece of lightweight water-
  soluble stabiliser eg Solvy

THREADS
> Stranded cotton
  Medium blue
  Light blue
> Variegated stranded cotton
  Medium blue

BEADS
> Crystal glass seed beads

EQUIPMENT
> 10cm (4") embroidery hoop
> Fine permanent pen
> No. 9 crewel needle

stitches & technique used

back stitch, page 115

beading, page 115

stem stitch, page 123

Getting started

See the liftout pattern sheet for the embroidery design.

- Place a scrap of fabric on your ironing board to protect it.
- Turn the top to the wrong side.
- Fuse the piece of interfacing to the wrong side of the top at the position for the embroidery, taking care not to stretch the fabric *(diag 1).*

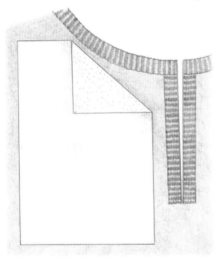

Diag 1

- Turn the top to the right side.

Transferring the design

- Using the pen, trace the design onto the water-soluble stabiliser (see page 19).
- Lay the top on a table and place a book or similar item inside it, behind the area which is to be embroidered. Position the tracing over the top. Tack in place close to the traced design, taking care not to stretch the fabric *(diag 2)*. Remove the book.

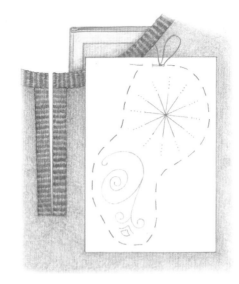

Diag 2

- Place the front of the top in the hoop, without stretching the knitted fabric (see page 21).
- You will need to move the hoop as you work because the design is so close to the neckline.

How to stitch the design

All embroidery is stitched with two strands of thread. When you are stitching with more than one strand, remember to strip the threads and keep them untwisted while you stitch (see page 17).

Order of work

Star

- Work every second spoke in stem stitch, using medium blue. Stab the needle through the fabric and keep the stitches short (see next page).
- Stitch the rest of the spokes in back stitch, using the lighter blue thread *(diag 3)*.

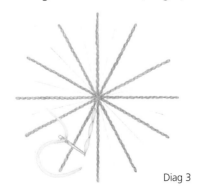

Diag 3

Swirls

Work the design below the star in stem stitch using the variegated thread. Work shorter stitches around the tight curves *(diag 4)*.

Diag 4

Remove the top from the hoop.

Beading

- Using a single strand of the medium blue, stitch a row of four beads in place above each dark spoke around the star *(diag 5)*.

Diag 5

- Secure the thread between each row of beads to avoid carrying the thread across the back of the work.

- Using the light blue thread, stitch rows of beads in place along the right hand side and below the swirl design in the same way.

Finishing

Remove the water-soluble stabiliser (see page 20).

On the wrong side, peel the interfacing back and trim carefully close to the embroidery (see diag 5, page 95).

WORKING STEM STITCH IN A STABBING MOTION

When stitching using a hoop, it is necessary to work in a stabbing motion instead of skimming the needle through the fabric, as shown in the step-by-step instructions on page 123. The difference is that you take the needle all the way through the fabric in each move, instead of in and out in one motion, as when you sew.

- Bring the thread to the front at the end of the line.

- Take the thread to the back at A, leaving a loop on the front *(fig 1)*.

Fig 1

- Bring the needle to the front at B, above the loop *(fig 2)*.

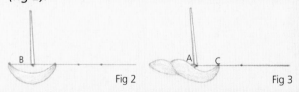

Fig 2

Fig 3

- Pull the thread through until the stitch rests on the fabric. Take the thread to the back at C. Leave a loop on the front and bring the needle to the front at A *(fig 3)*. Pull the thread through as before.

billy buttons

The buttons measure 22mm (7/8") in diameter.

YOU WILL NEED

FABRIC
> White cotton for three buttons

SUPPLIES
> 22mm (7/8") self-cover buttons

THREADS
> Stranded cotton
  Blue
  Orange
  Red
  Yellow

EQUIPMENT
> Tracing paper
> Fine black pen
> Fine water-soluble fabric marker
> No. 9 crewel

☺☺☺ **SUPER EASY**

Getting started

Transferring the embroidery design

- Use the water-soluble marker to trace the button template, supplied by the manufacturer, onto the fabric for the cutting line (see page 19).

- Trace the two circles below onto the tracing paper with the pen. Position the fabric over the tracing, centering the design inside the marked cutting line. Pin in place. Using the fabric marker, trace the circles onto the fabric.

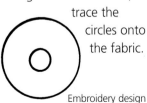

Embroidery design

How to stitch the daisy

Order of work

Petals

Using one strand, bring the needle to the front at the 12 o'clock point of the innermost circle *(diag 1)*.

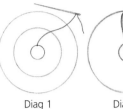

Diag 1   Diag 2

Work a detached chain, securing the stitch on the second circle for the first petal *(diag 2)*.

Stitch a petal at the 3, 6 and 9 o'clock points in the same manner *(diag 3)*.

Diag 3   Diag 4

Work another two petals in the spaces between the first petals *(diag 4)*.

Work a straight stitch inside each detached chain petal *(diag 5)*.

Centre

Using two strands of yellow, fill the centre of each flower with closely worked French knots, wrapping the thread around the needle twice for each knot *(diag 6)*.

Diag 5   Diag 6

Making the buttons

- Cut out each button cover along the cutting line.
- Rinse the pieces gently in cold water to remove any traced lines still showing. Leave the pieces to dry.
- Place the pieces with the wrong side facing up on a soft surface, eg a towel, and press.
- Make up the buttons following the manufacturer's instructions. Make sure the embroidery is centered over the button cap before you secure it, as it cannot be corrected once the button is complete.

stitches used

detached chain, page 121 | french knot, page 122 | straight stitch, page 124

safe sailing

How to make the key ring

Order of work

Legs

- Cut one 30cm (12") length of thread for each leg.
- Take one thread through two diagonal holes (A and B) in a black button and slide the button halfway along the thread. Take one thread tail through the remaining button holes (C and D), to form a cross on the front *(diag 1)*. Take the other tail through D and C *(diag 2)*.

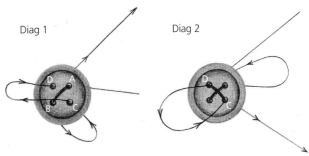

Diag 1　　　　　Diag 2

- Bring the pair of threads through two blue oval beads to form a leg *(diag 3)*. Repeat for the second leg. Set the legs aside.

Arms

- Cut one 30cm (12") length of thread for each arm.
- Position a small natural wooden bead halfway along one thread. Double the thread over.
- Bring the doubled thread through two red oval beads to form an arm *(diag 4)*. Repeat for the second arm.

Diag 3　　　Diag 4

KEY RING
YOU WILL NEED

SUPPLIES

> 2cm (³/4") key ring
> 6mm (¹/4") ring

BUTTONS

> 4 x 15mm (⁵/8") white two-hole buttons
> 4 x 15mm (⁵/8") red two-hole buttons
> 2 x 10mm (³/8") black four-hole buttons

BEADS

> 1 x 10mm (³/8") natural wooden bead
> 1 x 4mm (³/16") red wooden bead
> 3 x 6mm (¹/4") natural wooden beads
> 4 x 15mm (⁵/8") red oval wooden beads
> 4 x 15mm (⁵/8") blue oval wooden beads

EQUIPMENT

> Long-nose pliers
> Black buttonhole thread
> No. 9 milliner's needle

Body

- Beginning with a red button, take the threads from one leg through one hole of each of the six buttons, alternating red with white. Bring the threads from the second leg through the other hole in the buttons *(diag 5)*.

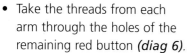

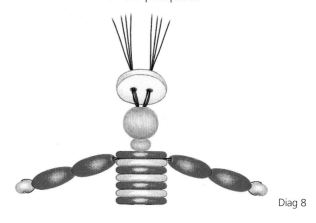

- Take the threads from each arm through the holes of the remaining red button *(diag 6)*.

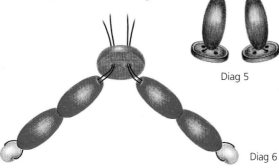

Diag 5

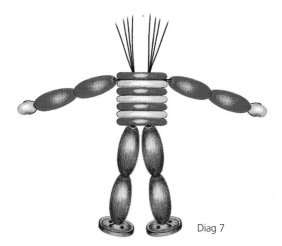

Diag 6

- Bring the threads from the legs and body through the red button, adjusting the arms, so the button sits flat against the body *(diag 7)*.

Diag 7

Head and beret

- Group all the threads together and bring them through the remaining small wooden bead and the large wooden bead to form the neck and head.

- Divide the threads into two even groups and take each group through a hole in the remaining white button *(diag 8)*. Take all the threads through the small red bead for the pompom.

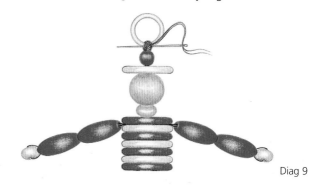

Diag 8

Attaching the key ring

- Tie the threads securely to the small ring with a double knot. Stitch each tail through the knot two or three times to secure *(diag 9)*. Trim the tails.

- Slide the small ring onto the keyring.

Diag 9

The key ring measures 10cm (4") long.

The bag measures
28cm x 22cm wide
(11" x 8 5/8").

SHOULDER BAG
YOU WILL NEED

FABRIC

> 35cm x 85cm wide
  (13 3/4" x 33 1/2") piece of
  navy blue linen (bag)
> 35cm x 85cm wide
  (13 3/4" x 33 1/2") piece of
  red and white striped cotton
  (lining)
> Cotton fabrics for appliqué
  Navy and white spot
  Pale peach
  Red
  White

SUPPLIES

> Large white button
> Red button
> 4mm (3/16") red wooden bead
> 1.7m (1yd 31") length of red
  and white cord
> Navy machine sewing thread
> Appliqué paper

THREADS

> Stranded cotton
  Christmas red
  Medium brown
  Navy blue
  Very light peach
  White

EQUIPMENT

> 13cm (5") embroidery hoop
> Tracing paper
> Dressmaker's carbon paper
> Fine black permanent pen
> No. 7 and no. 9 crewel
  needles

**This project requires
machine sewing**

Getting started

See the liftout pattern sheet for the embroidery design and appliqué templates.

Cutting out

Cut the navy linen to 24cm x 76cm wide (9 1/2" x 30"), cutting along the grain of the fabric (see page 10).

Preparing the fabric for embroidery

- Neaten the raw edges with a machine zigzag or overlock stitch to prevent the fabric from fraying while you stitch.

- Fold the fabric in half along the length and finger press the fold lightly. Unfold the fabric. Measure 29cm (11 3/8") from one end along the foldline. At this point, fold the fabric across the width and finger press as before. This marks the centre of the design *(diag 1)*.

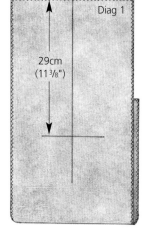

Diag 1

29cm
(11 3/8")

Transferring and preparing the sailor

- Using the pen, trace the design and placement marks onto tracing paper. Aligning the placement marks with the fold lines, transfer it onto the linen, using the dressmaker's carbon (see page 19).

- Prepare the appliqué pieces following steps 1 - 3 of the instructions on pages 113 and 114.

- Remove the appliqué paper from each foot piece and lightly fuse in place overlapping the lower edge of the pants *(diag 2)*.

Diag 2   Diag 3

- Continue to fuse the pieces for the sailor in place in numerical order. Overlap the pieces so each follows the marked outlines *(diag 3)*.

How to stitch the sailor

Use the no. 7 needle when stitching with four strands of thread and the no. 9 needle for all other stitching.

Work the embroidery with the fabric held taut in the hoop, working the stitches in a stabbing motion (see page 21).

Order of work

Sailor

Use two strands of matching thread to work the blanket stitch around the appliqué pieces.

Stitch around the pieces in the reverse order to the order of fusing.

- Begin by stitching around the sack, working three stitches into the same hole in the fabric at the corners *(diag 4)*.

Diag 4

- Work blanket stitch around the beret.
- Continue to work blanket stitch over the edges of the remaining appliqué pieces in the same way.
- The edge of the blanket stitches around the pants and beret are whipped using two strands of white.

Bring the white thread to the front very close to the blanket stitch *(diag 5)*.

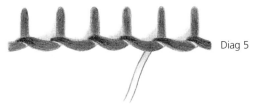

Diag 5

Take the needle over the blanket stitch and slide the eye end under the next stitch from the opposite side *(diag 6)*.

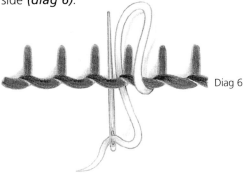

Diag 6

Continue to whip into each blanket stitch around the edge *(diag 7)*.

Diag 7

- Using a sharp pencil, lightly draw the shape for the sleeve onto the shirt *(diag 8)*. Work a row of back stitch along the line with two strands of navy thread.

Diag 8

Stick

Work the stick in back stitch using four strands of brown in the large needle.

Face

Stitch a French knot for each eye, using one strand of brown. Work a loose straight stitch for the mouth with a single strand of red. Work a tiny stitch over the straight stitch to make it curve slightly *(diag 9)*.

Diag 9

Pompom

Using the red thread, stitch the bead securely in place above the beret for the pompom.

How to make the shoulder bag

See page 106 for instructions.

The sailor measures 7.5cm x 6.5cm wide (3" x 2 ½").

daisy chain

stitch used

detached chain, page 121

 **SUPER EASY**

YOU WILL NEED

SUPPLIES
> Small drawstring bag

THREADS
> Stranded cotton
  Dark yellow
  Light olive green
  Medium olive green
  Orange
  Red
  Yellow

EQUIPMENT
> Dressmaker's carbon
  paper
> Fine ball point pen
> No. 8 crewel needle

Getting started

See the liftout pattern sheet for the embroidery design.

Fold the bag in half along the length and lightly finger press the fold to mark the centre (*diag 1*). Unfold the bag.

Transferring the design

Centre the design along the lower edge of the bag and transfer the daisies using the carbon paper (see page 19).

Diag 1

How to stitch the daisies

All embroidery is stitched with three strands of thread. Strip the threads and keep them untwisted while you work (see page 17).

Order of work

Daisies

- Stitch the large red daisy first. Secure the thread with a knot and work the eight detached chain petals. Bring the needle to the front just outside the marked centre for each stitch to avoid crowding the stitches (*diag 2*).

Diag 2

- Work an orange daisy on each side of the red daisy in the same way.

- Stitch two yellow daisies next to each orange daisy, working six detached chain petals for each and using the lighter shade for the smallest daisies (*diag 3*).

Diag 3

Leaves

The leaves are also embroidered in detached chain, some with the darker shade of olive green and some with the lighter.

To make a pointier stitch, you will need to anchor each chain with a longer stitch by taking the needle to the back a short distance from the loop (*diags 4 & 5*).

Diag 4   Diag 5

The daisy border measures 3.5cm x 10.8cm wide (1 ³/₄" x 4 ¹/₈").

circles & stripes

CUSHION WITH STRIPES
YOU WILL NEED

SUPPLIES
> Cream cushion
> A selection of buttons in various sizes to complement your cushion

THREADS
> No. 5 perlé cotton
  Grey-green
> Stranded cotton
  Light grey

EQUIPMENT
> Water-soluble fabric marker
> Ruler
> Magic tape (optional)
> No. 4 and no. 7 crewel needles

stitch & technique used

attaching buttons, page 111

running stitch, page 122

CUSHION WITH CIRCLES
YOU WILL NEED

SUPPLIES
> Mocha cushion

THREADS
> No. 5 perlé cotton
  Light beige
> Stranded cotton
  Beige
  Rust

BEADS
> 4mm (3/16") hazelnut wooden beads
> 6mm (1/4") natural wooden beads
> 8mm (5/16") natural oval wooden beads

EQUIPMENT
> Water-soluble fabric marker
> No. 4 and no. 7 crewel needles

stitch & technique used

beading, page 115

chain stitch, page 120

 **SUPER EASY**

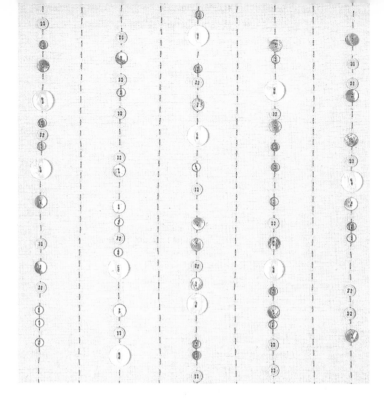

Getting started

Remove the cushion insert from the cover.

Placing the designs

Cushion with stripes

- Measure across the width to find the centre of the cushion cover.

- Using the fabric marker and ruler, rule a line down the length *(diag 1)*.

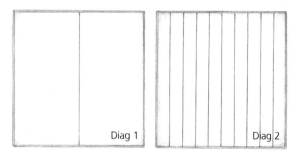

Diag 1   Diag 2

- Rule parallel lines at 4cm (1 ½") intervals on each side of the centre line *(diag 2)*.

Cushion with circles

- Choose a selection of plates, saucers, cups and glasses, all different sizes, to use as templates for the circles (see page 19). You will need four or five different sizes.

- Use the fabric marker to trace around the kitchen items. You can use the photograph as a guide for the placement of the circles.

How to stitch the designs

Use two strands of thread to attach the beads and buttons. When you are stitching with more than one strand of thread, remember to strip the threads and keep them untwisted while you stitch (see page 17).

Use the no. 4 crewel needle when working the chain stitch and running stitch and the no. 7 for attaching the beads and buttons.

Order of work

Cushion with stripes

- Work running stitch along each ruled line, using grey-green perlé cotton. To get the best effect, try and keep the stitches as even as possible in length using magic tape (see hint).

- Once all the lines are stitched, place the cover flat on a table. Arrange your selection of buttons over every second line of stitching. When you are happy with the arrangement, lift each row of buttons onto the table. It might seem a little tedious to have to do this, but it is the best way to place the buttons back on the cushion cover in the right order.

- Stitch each button in place with two strands of grey thread, keeping the stitches parallel to the running stitch beneath *(diag 3)*.

Diag 3

KEEPING IT EVEN

To achieve nice even stitches you can use magic tape as a guide. Place a length of tape along the line you are about to stitch and use a ruler to mark the length of the stitches onto the tape. Stitch using the edge and marks on the tape as a guide (see diag 3, page 55).

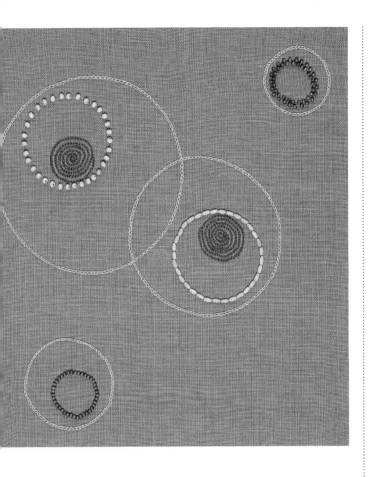

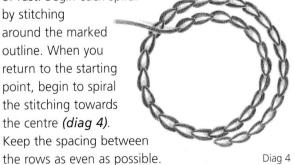

Cushion with circles

- Stitch each outer circle in chain stitch, using the beige perlé thread.

- The spirals in the smallest circles are worked in chain stitch, using three strands of rust. Begin each spiral by stitching around the marked outline. When you return to the starting point, begin to spiral the stitching towards the centre *(diag 4)*. Keep the spacing between the rows as even as possible.

Diag 4

- Stitch the large round beads in place, spacing them one bead's width apart and taking the thread through each bead twice (see page 115).

- Stitch the double row of small hazelnut beads in place in the same way, off-setting the beads in the inner circle *(diag 5)*.

Diag 5

- Attach the hazelnut and oval beads with back stitch around the last two circles (see page 116).

Finishing

Rinse the cushion cover in cold water to remove any traces of the fabric marker. Leave to dry and press from the wrong side, avoiding the beads and buttons.

. . . .

JOINING A NEW THREAD IN CHAIN STITCH

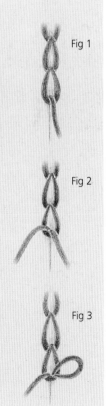

Fig 1

Fig 2

Fig 3

It can be very frustrating to have to join a new thread part way through your stitching, but with this little hint the join will be seamless.

- Remove the needle from the old thread, leaving the tail hanging inside the last chain *(fig 1)*.

- Secure the new thread on the back and bring it to the front at the same point as the old thread tail *(fig 2)*.

- Rethread the old tail into the needle and take it to the back through the same hole in the fabric *(fig 3)*.

The last chain is now anchored around the new thread.

pebbles

YOU WILL NEED

SUPPLIES
> Skirt
> Magic tape

THREADS
> No. 5 perlé cotton
  Dark navy

EQUIPMENT
> Ruler
> Sharp pencil
> No. 5 crewel needle

stitch used

french knot, page 122

DRESS UP A SKIRT IN A DASH

If time is of the essence and you want to decorate your skirt quickly, try working even rows of running stitches instead of French knots.

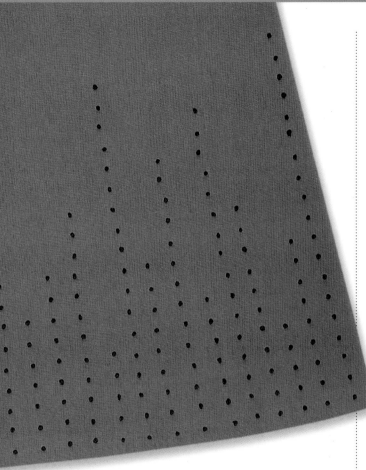

How to stitch the border

- Starting 1.5cm (⁵/₈") from the hem, mark the tape at 1.5cm (⁵/₈") intervals using the pencil *(diag 3)*.

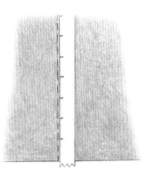

Diag 3   Diag 4

- Stitch a French knot at the edge of the tape at each of the marked positions *(diag 4)*.

- Remove the tape.

- At the lower edge, measure 2cm (³/₄") to one side of the first knot. Reposition the tape at this point, at a right angle to the lower edge.

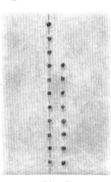

- Stitch the knots in the same way as the first row, changing the length of the row *(diag 5)*.

Diag 5

- Prepare a new length of tape when necessary. Stitch each row of knots in the same way, varying the length of the rows and making sure each is at a right angle to the edge of the skirt.

Getting started

- Fold the skirt, in half with wrong sides together and matching side seams, to find the centre front and back *(diag 1)*.

   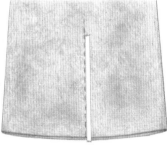

Diag 1   Diag 2

- Press the folds lightly with your fingers. Lay the skirt flat and place a 30cm (12") length of tape along the back and front folds *(diag 2)*.

STAYING STRAIGHT

It is important that each row of knots is at a right angle to the hem, otherwise you could end up with uneven rows that are leaning to one side. If the hem of your skirt is curved, it can be helpful to use a set square to make sure the tape is at a right angle to the edge.

Lay the skirt flat at regular intervals and look at it from a distance to make sure the rows all point towards the waist.

let it snow

 **VERY EASY**

YOU WILL NEED

FABRIC
> 37cm x 139cm wide (14 1/2" x 54 3/4") piece of cream medium weight furnishing fabric
> 20cm (8") square of slate grey medium weight cotton

SUPPLIES
> Photo album 33cm x 26cm wide (13" x 10 1/4")

THREADS
> Stranded cotton
  Copper
  Ecru
  Ochre
> No. 5 perlé cotton
  Very light tan

BEADS
> Cream glass seed beads

EQUIPMENT
> Tracing paper
> Fine black pen
> Dressmaker's carbon paper
> No. 7 and no. 9 crewel needles

This project requires machine sewing

Getting started

See the liftout pattern sheet for the embroidery design.

Fold the grey cotton into quarters along the straight grain of the fabric (see page 10). Finger press the folds to mark the centre.

Transferring the design

Transfer the design onto the centre of the cotton using the dressmaker's carbon paper (see page 19). You don't need to transfer the dots. The beads and French knots are very easy to stitch without marking.

WHAT IF MY PHOTO ALBUM IS A DIFFERENT SIZE?

The embroidered patch on the front of the cover can be used no matter what size your album is. You can easily change the measurements for the cover (see page 107).

How to stitch the design

When you stitch with more than one strand of thread, strip the threads and keep them untwisted while you work (see page 17).

Use the small needle and one strand of ecru to attach the beads and the larger needle for all other stitching.

Order of work

Tree

Stitch the outline of the tree in stem stitch with three strands of ecru. To join a new thread when working stem stitch see the hint on page 104.

Apples

- Work the stems for the apples in back stitch using three strands of ecru as before.
- Stitch a blanket stitch wheel for each apple, using two strands of thread. Embroider some apples with ochre, some with copper and some with one strand of each shade in the needle *(diag 1)*.

Diag 1

Snow

- Using one strand of ecru, stitch the beads in place, scattered above and around the tree.
- Stitch French knots randomly among the beads using one or two strands of ecru. Add a few knots in ochre or copper thread.

How to attach the embroidery

- Trim the embroidered fabric to 15cm (6") square, cutting along the grain of the fabric.

- Use a needle to ease out the fabric threads along each side to make the fringe *(diag 2)*.

Press the embroidered piece (see page 22).

- Fold the furnishing fabric across the width 49.5cm (19 1/2") from the left hand side and finger press the fold. Unfold the fabric. Centre the embroidery

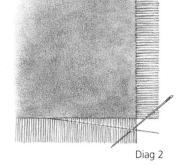

Diag 2

over the foldline, halfway between the upper and lower edge, and pin it in place *(diag 3)*.

- Stitch the piece in place with running stitch around the edge using perlé thread *(diag 4)*.

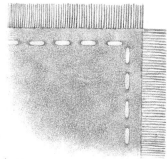

Diag 3

Making the album cover

See page 107 for instructions.

Diag 4

MIXING COLOURS

You can easily create variegated threads and subtle colour variations by stitching with two or three different colours of thread in the needle.

TURNING A SHARP CORNER IN STEM STITCH

To create a point or corner in stem stitch, the beginning and end of the rows should be worked through the same hole in the fabric. Because of the nature of the stitch, this is impossible to do without securing the thread.

- Finish the row of stitches at the point *(fig 1)*.

Fig 1

- Turn the work to the wrong side and slide the needle under the last stitch on the back *(fig 2)*. Pull the thread through to anchor the thread.

Fig 2

- Return the needle and thread to the front through the same hole in the fabric at the point *(fig 3)*. You can now continue the stem stitch.

Fig 3

This album measures 33cm x 26cm wide (13" x 10 1/4").
The embroidered patch measures 15cm (6") square.

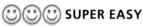
autumn leaves

stitch used

running stitch, page 122

Getting started

See the liftout pattern sheet for the embroidery design.

Measure and mark the centre of the blind along the lower edge.

Transferring the design

• Transfer the design and placement marks onto the tracing paper using the black pen.

• Position the tracing behind one half of the blind, aligning the centre marks. The lower edge of the tracing should be approximately 4cm (1½") from the lower edge of the blind. Tape the tracing in place *(diag 1)*.

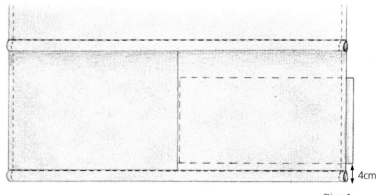

4cm

Diag 1

YOU WILL NEED

SUPPLIES
> Cream Roman blind

THREADS
> No. 5 perlé cotton
> Honey
> Straw
> Very pale yellow

EQUIPMENT
> Tracing paper
> Fine black pen
> Fine water-soluble fabric marker
> No. 5 crewel needle

- Trace the design onto the blind over a window or lightbox, using the fabric marker (see page 18).
- Flip the tracing and transfer the border onto the second half of the blind in the same way.

WHAT IF MY BLIND IS WIDER?

You can extend the pattern, or a portion of it, to each side of the blind as many times as necessary to fill the full width. Flip the tracing for each repeat and always begin from the centre of your blind.

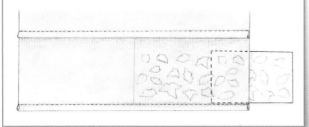

How to stitch the leaves

For this design it is important that you have the right amount of thread to stitch all the way around a leaf without running out. To make sure your thread is long enough, lay it around the leaf you are about to stitch. Double this length before you cut *(diag 2)*.

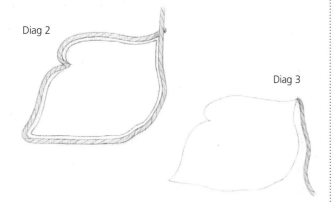

Diag 2

Diag 3

- Take the needle to the back at the base of a leaf, leaving a 5cm (2") tail of thread on the front *(diag 3)*.

- Work small running stitches around the shape of the leaf.
- Adjust the stitches as you near the starting point to make sure you finish with the thread on the front *(diag 4)*.

Diag 4

- Unthread the needle. Tie the two thread tails in a loose knot. To make it easier to position the knot on the fabric, place the tip of the needle inside the loop of the knot and hold it on the fabric before pulling the knot tight around the needle *(diag 5)*.

Diag 5

- Trim the tails 1.5cm (⅝") from the fabric.
- Stitch all the leaves in this way, varying the shade of thread. Make sure you use the same colour thread for the same leaf on each half of the border.

Finishing

Rinse the embroidered section of the blind in cold water to remove any traces of the fabric marker (see page 18). Squeeze as much moisture as possible out of the blind with a towel and hang it up to dry.

CREATE YOUR OWN LEAF DESIGN

It is very easy to create your own leaf design. All you need is a garden or park from which to pick a selection of leaves. Bring them home and arrange on a piece of paper which is half as wide as your blind. Once you are happy with the arrangement, hold each leaf in place with a little glue or tape. You can scan the arrangement into your computer and print the design or make a photocopy. Trace the outlines of the leaves onto tracing paper with a black pen and there is your design ready to be transferred onto your blind, cushion, wrap, apron or bag. The options are endless.

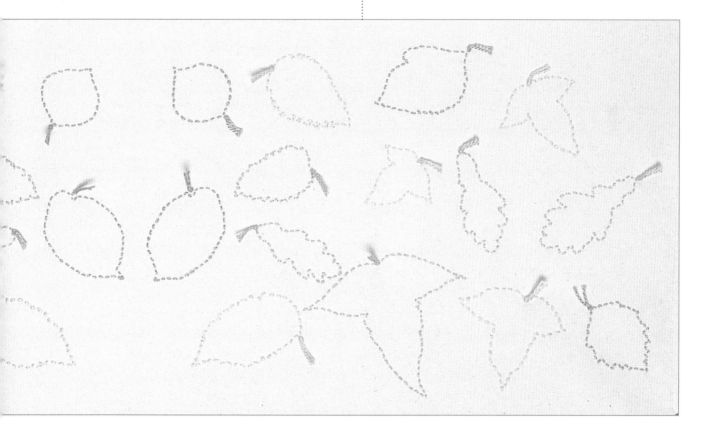

YOU WILL NEED

FABRIC
> Small piece of dark beige cotton
> Small piece of burnt orange cotton

SUPPLIES
> White body suit
> Cream jacket or cardigan
> Appliqué paper

THREADS
> Stranded cotton
   Coral
   Mahogany
   Navy blue
   Ochre
   White

EQUIPMENT
> Tissue paper
> Dressmaker's carbon paper
> Fine black pen
> Sharp pencil
> No. 9 crewel needle

stitches used

blanket stitch, page 118

detached chain, page 121

french knot, page 122

running stitch, page 122

straight stitch, page 124

technique used

appliqué, page 113

☺☺☺ **VERY EASY**

kitty kat

Getting started

See the liftout pattern sheet for the embroidery designs and appliqué templates.

Body suit

• Cut a 4.5cm (1 3/4") square of dark beige cotton, cutting along the grain of the fabric (see page 10).

Diag 1

Cut a 2.5cm (1 3/8") square of appliqué paper.

• Centre the appliqué paper, with the smooth side facing up, on the wrong side of the fabric square and fuse in place *(diag 1)*.

Diag 2

• Use a needle to gently ease out the fabric threads for 5mm (1/4") on each side of the square to make the fringe *(diag 2)*.

• Remove the paper backing and fuse the fabric patch in place at the centre front of the body suit.

• Transfer the face of the cat onto the patch using dress maker's carbon (see page 19).

Jacket

- Prepare the appliqué pieces (see page 113).
- Using the close-up photograph as a guide, fuse the cat and bird pieces in place on the left hand side of the jacket.
- Lightly draw the cat's face and spots using a sharp pencil, or transfer the lines using dressmaker's carbon as before.

How to stitch the cat

When you are stitching with more than one strand of thread, remember to strip the threads and keep them untwisted while you stitch (see page 17).

Order of work

Body suit

- Work the outline of the cat's face and ears in back stitch, using two strands of mahogany.
- Beginning at one corner, work running stitch around the edge of the patch, 2mm (1/16") from the fringe, with two strands of ochre. Add a diagonal stitch over the edge of the patch at each corner *(diag 3)*.

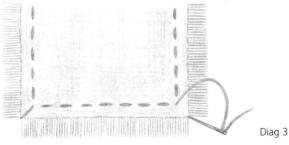

Diag 3

- Using one strand of navy and beginning with the longest stitch at the upper edge, stitch a small triangle for the nose with parallel straight stitches *(diag 4)*. Embroider the mouth in back stitch.

Diag 4

- With one strand of white, work two small crossed straight stitches at the position for one eye *(diag 5)*.

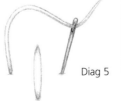

Diag 5

Work a second pair of crossed stitches over and between the first *(diag 6)*.
Repeat for the other eye.

Stitch a French knot at the centre of each eye, using two strands of navy *(diag 7)*.

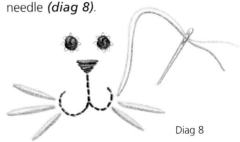

Diag 6   Diag 7

- Work three long straight stitches on each side of the face for the whiskers, using one strand of mahogany and one strand of ochre together in the needle *(diag 8)*.

Diag 8

- Using two strands of ochre, stitch French knots at short intervals along the neckline seam. If you skim the needle between the layers of fabric between each knot, you avoid the stitches showing on the back *(diag 9)*.

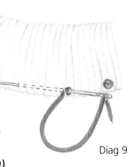

Diag 9

LOOSEN UP
Be careful that you don't pull the thread tight between the knots or you will lose the stretch in the fabric and the garment will be difficult to get over baby's head.

Jacket

Cat

- Beginning above the head, work blanket stitch over the edge of the fabric around the cat's body, tail and legs, using one strand of mahogany.

Stitch around the head and ears in the same way, working three stitches into the same hole in the fabric at the tip of each ear *(diag 10)*.

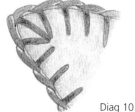

Diag 10

- Using two strands of mahogany, stitch a detached chain for each spot. Using two strands of ochre, work a French knot inside each detached chain *(diag 11)*.

Diag 11

- Embroider the cat's face in the same way as described for the patch on the romper.

Birds

- Using two strands of coral, work three detached chains over the tip of the body shape for the tail. To have a nicely fanned tail, work the centre stitch first, followed by a stitch on each side *(diag 12)*.

Diag 12

- Bring the needle to the front through the appliquéd fabric and work a detached chain over the edge of the fabric for one wing. Stitch the second wing from the upper edge of the appliqué piece *(diag 13)*.

Diag 13

- Stitch the legs, beak and eye with two strands of navy. Work each leg with a long straight stitch over the edge of the fabric shape. Work two straight stitches into the same hole at the tip for the beak *(diag 14)*.

Finish each bird with a French knot for the eye.

Diag 14

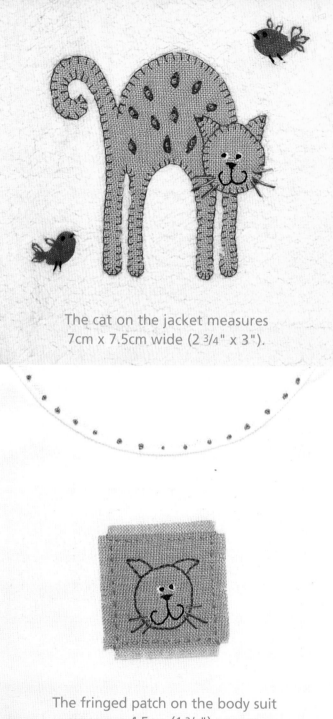

The cat on the jacket measures 7cm x 7.5cm wide (2 3/4" x 3").

The fringed patch on the body suit measures 4.5cm (1 3/4") square.

DON'T LIKE CATS?

If you are not a cat person, colouring-in books are great for finding simple shapes to use for appliqué. You could also use the little sailor on page 46 or simple flowers like those on the jeans on page 26.

YOU WILL NEED

FABRIC

> 10cm x 12cm wide (4" x 4 ³/₄")
> piece of white felt
> 10cm x 20cm wide (4" x 8")
> piece of ochre felt
> 5cm x 10cm wide (2" x 4")
> piece of dark beige felt
> 12cm x 15cm wide (4 ³/₄" x 6")
> piece of brown felt

SUPPLIES

> 15cm (6") embroidery hoop,
> inner ring only
> 3m (3yd 10") white piping cord,
> size 0
> Appliqué paper
> Fibre-fill

THREADS

> Stranded cotton
> Copper
> Dark beige
> Dark navy blue
> Ochre
> No. 5 perlé cotton
> Beige
> Copper
> Dark chocolate
> White

RIBBONS

> 15cm x 7mm wide (6" x ⁵/₁₆")
> blue silk ribbon
> 15cm x 7mm wide (6" x ⁵/₁₆")
> green silk ribbon
> 15cm x 7mm wide (6" x ⁵/₁₆")
> burgundy silk ribbon

EQUIPMENT

> Lightweight card
> Fine black pen
> Sharp pencil
> No. 9 crewel needle
> No. 9 sharp needle

curious
cats

back stitch, page 115

blanket stitch, page 118

blanket stitch pinwheel, page 119

chain stitch, page 120

french knot, page 122

straight stitch, page 124

technique used

twisted cord, page 112

Getting started

See the liftout pattern sheet for the templates and embroidery designs.

In this project the appliqué paper is used to make it easier to cut the felt pieces accurately.

- Using the pencil, trace the templates for the heads and bodies onto the smooth side of the appliqué paper, marking the position for the cord on the upper edge of each body piece.

  Use a warm, dry iron to fuse the tracings onto the appropriate colours of felt and cut out along the traced lines.

- Lift the paper backing along the top edge of a body piece for each cat and transfer the mark for the cord onto the back of the felt with the pencil *(diag 1)*. Remove the paper backing.

  Diag 1

- Make a card template for the ear and trace onto the pieces of felt with the pen (see page 19). Cut out each ear piece just inside the traced line.

- Cut six circles 6mm (¹/₄") in diameter from the white felt for the eyes.

 **VERY EASY**

How to transfer the faces and body markings

Face

The faces are stitched in a similar way to the cat on the baby body suit on page 66. It can be difficult to transfer onto felt, so use the photograph as a guide and draw each face very lightly with the pencil.

- Mark the top of the nose with a dot just below the centre of the face and draw a curl for each side of the mouth *(diag 2)*. The eyes do not need to be marked.

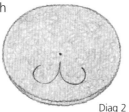

Diag 2

Body

Lightly draw four or five circles of different sizes on each of the white body pieces and draw uneven lines for the stripes on the two ochre pieces. The dots on the brown cat do not need to be marked.

How to stitch the design

Use the sharp needle for the blanket stitch around the edges of each cat and the crewel needle for all other stitching. When you work with more than one strand of thread, remember to strip the threads and keep them untwisted (see page 17).

Order of work

Faces

- Using two strands of navy and starting with a long straight stitch over the marked dot, stitch a small triangle for the nose with parallel straight stitches *(diag 3)*. Embroider the mouth in back stitch.

Diag 3

- Position a felt eye piece just above and to one side of the nose and hold it in place with your hand. Stitch the eye in place with a French knot at the centre *(diag 4)*.

Diag 4

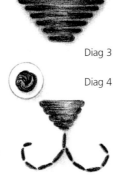

Dotty the brown cat

The dots are stitched in French knots using copper perlé thread or three strands of ochre.

- Work the copper knots, first spacing them randomly over each body shape. Fill in all the spaces with ochre knots.
- Stitch a few dots on the back of the head in the same way.

Spotty the white cat

Work each spot with a blanket stitch pinwheel, using three strands of dark beige thread.

Stripey the ochre cat

- Stitch the stripes in chain stitch with three strands of copper. Begin each row at the top and zigzag the stitches from side to side across the marked line *(diags 5 and 6)*.

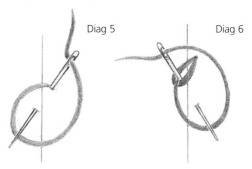

Diag 5   Diag 6

- Work three short stripes from the top edge of the back head piece in the same way.

How to make the cats

All three cats are made in the same way, using a single strand of cotton for the blanket stitch edges.

Legs and tail

- Cut a 1m (1yd 3 3/8") length of perlé thread for each leg and tail.
- Make a twisted cord from each piece (see page 112). Set the three tail pieces aside and knot each leg piece 4cm (1 1/2") from the folded end and trim *(diag 7)*.

Diag 7

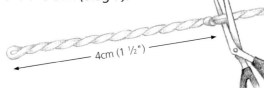

4cm (1 1/2")

Head

- Place the back head piece behind the back body piece and stitch in place with blanket stitch along the edge (*diag 8*).

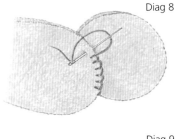

Diag 8

- Tack each ear in place behind the face piece with several small stitches (*diag 9*).

Diag 9

- Place the face over the body front and stitch in place in a similar way to the back, beginning at the top.

Joining the front and back

- Cut the piping cord into three even lengths and knot each end of each piece.

- Position the front of the cat over the back with wrong sides together and matching edges. Place a twisted cord between the layers at the marked position on the cat's back and hold it in place with a pin (*diag 10*).

Diag 10

- Begin at the neck and work blanket stitch over the edges of the felt to join the front and back head pieces (*diag 11*).

Diag 11

- Place the folded end of the leg pieces and the knotted end of the tail between the layers and stitch securely in place. Continue along the back, stitching the cord securely in place as you work.

- Push a small amount of fibre-fill into the head and body just before you complete the stitching, but take care not to over fill the cats.

Bow

Tie a length of ribbon in a small bow and trim the tails. Stitch the bow securely in place under the cat's chin.

Attaching the cats to the ring

- Wrap the cord from one cat twice around the hoop ring. Adjust the cord length and tie a knot on the inside of the ring.

- Repeat for the other two cats placing the cords evenly around the ring.

- Bring the cord ends together at the top and tie in a knot.

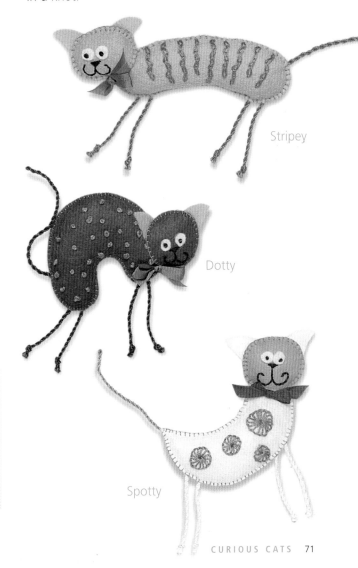

Stripey

Dotty

Spotty

The finished lantern measures 11.5cm (4 1/2") high and 23cm (9") in circumference.

twilight

stitches & techniques used

attaching sequins, page 117

back stitch, page 115

beading, page 115

detached chain, page 121

straight stitch, page 124

Preparing the paper for embroidery

See the liftout pattern sheet for the embroidery design and pattern.

- Using the sharp white pencil trace the design and cutting lines onto the drafting paper. Use a ruler for the straight lines.
- Cut out the paper along the marked cutting lines.

What if my tumbler is a different size?

- Measure around your tumbler. Adjust the length of the design and add 6mm (1/4") to this measurement to allow for the drafting paper to overlap.
- Measure the height of your glass and adjust the height of the design to fit this measurement.

YOU WILL NEED

SUPPLIES
- Drafting paper
- White beading thread
- Straight sided glass tumbler 11.5cm x 23cm in circumference (4 1/2" x 9")

BEADS & SEQUINS
- 6mm (1/4") pearl cup sequins
- Mixed pastel coloured seed beads
- Size 8 clear beads
- Fuchsia bugle beads

EQUIPMENT
- Sharp white pencil
- Double-sided tape
- No. 10 sharp needle

 **VERY EASY**

How to stitch the design

It is important to avoid pulling the stitches too tight because the thread can easily tear the paper.

Order of work

Stem and leaves

- Knot the end of the thread and bring it to the front close to one short end.
- Work a straight stitch for the stem and re-emerge, leaving only a very short stitch on the wrong side of the paper *(diag 1)*.

Diag 1   Diag 2

- Stitch a detached chain for the first leaf. Bring the thread to the front at the base of the stitch *(diag 2)*.
- Continue working straight stitches with detached chain leaves at the marked positions until you reach the opposite end *(diag 3)*.

Diag 3

Knot the thread securely around the stitches on the back *(diag 4)*.

Tendrils

- Beginning at the stem, work back stitch along the tendril, keeping the stitches short to achieve a nice curve.

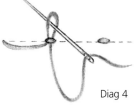

Diag 4

- Bring the needle to the front at the end of the tendril and thread on a large clear bead. Take a stitch over one side of the bead and re-emerge through the centre. Take a stitch over the opposite side of the bead *(diag 5)*. Tie off securely on the back, behind the bead.

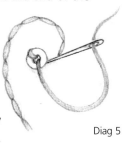

Diag 5

Flowers

- Knot and secure the thread at the main stem and stitch each flower stem in the same way as the tendrils.
- Stitch around the circle for the flower in running stitch, threading a pastel coloured bead onto the needle for each stitch *(diag 6)*.

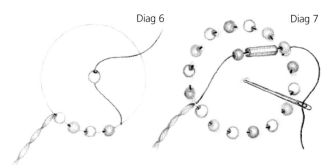

Diag 6   Diag 7

- At the base of the flower, thread a pink bead, followed by a bugle bead and a blue bead, onto the needle. Take the needle to the back through the centre of the flower *(diag 7)*. Secure the thread under the stem of the flower and trim.

Sequin borders

- Stitch a row of sequins in place with back stitch along the three marked lines.

EMBROIDERING ON PAPER

The revival of paper crafts, such as scrapbooking, has brought with it a renewed interest in embroidery on paper. Most of the beautiful papers available can be used for stitching to create greeting cards, gift tags, scrapbook pages and even picture frames. You can use the same threads and stitches as for other embroidery, but you will not have to worry about fraying edges or puckering. The only thing you need to watch out for is pulling your stitches too tight as the thread might tear the paper.

How to make the lantern

- On the right side of the paper, place a 6mm (¹/₄") wide piece of double-sided tape along one end *(diag 8)*.

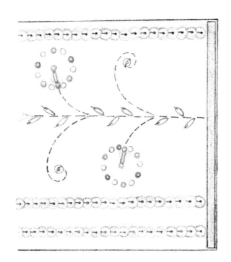

Diag 8

- Remove the paper backing from the tape. Place it over the opposite side of the paper to form a tube. Make sure the upper and lower edges, as well as the embroidery, line up at the join *(diag 9)*.

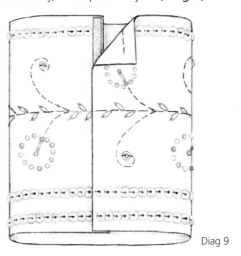

Diag 9

- Slide the lantern over the tumbler.

marigolds

YOU WILL NEED

FABRIC
> 100cm x 105cm wide
  (39 3/8" x 41 3/8") piece of natural
  coloured linen or cotton

SUPPLIES
> Matching machine sewing thread

THREADS
> Stranded cotton
  Light green-grey
  Medium green-grey
> No. 8 perlé cotton
  Honey
  Light tan
  Orange
  Straw
  White

EQUIPMENT
> Dressmaker's carbon paper
> Lightweight card
> Ruler
> Tracing paper
> Fine black pen
> Water-soluble fabric marker
> No. 8 crewel needle

**This project requires
machine sewing**

stitches used

blanket stitch, page 118

detached chain, page 121

french knot, page 122

running stitch, page 122

 EASY

Getting started

See the liftout pattern sheet for the embroidery design and leaf template.

Wash and press the fabric before you begin (see page 16).

Cutting out

Cut the pieces for the bag, lining and drawstrings according to the measurements below.

Bag and lining, cut two pieces, each 42cm x 82cm wide (16 1/2" x 32 1/4")

Drawstrings, cut two pieces, each 90cm x 6cm wide (35 1/2" x 2 3/8")

Cutting layout

1. Bag and lining
2. Drawstrings

Preparing the fabric for embroidery

- Neaten the raw edges of the piece for the bag with a machine zigzag or overlock stitch to prevent the fabric from fraying while you stitch.

- Fold the fabric in half down the length and finger press the fold. Unfold the fabric. Measure 22cm (8 5/8") from one end along the foldline. At this point, fold the fabric across the width and finger press as before *(diag 1)*.

Diag 1

Transferring the design

- Align the placement marks for the design with the foldlines and transfer the design using the dressmaker's carbon (see page 19).

- Rule an 8cm (3 1/8") line below each flower for the stem, using the water-soluble fabric marker.

- Make a leaf template from the card and mark the leaves along the stems (see page 19).

How to stitch the flowers

Use the close-up photograph as a guide for colour placement. When you stitch with more than one strand of thread, strip the threads and keep them untwisted (see page 17).

Order of work

Stems and leaves

The stems and leaves are worked in running stitch, using either two strands of light green-grey or medium green-grey.

- Keeping the stitches small and even, embroider each stem from the base to the top.

- Beginning near the stem, stitch around the leaves *(diag 2)*.

Diag 2

Flower one

- Using the straw coloured thread, stitch the inner circle in blanket stitch. To finish the circle, take the needle under the first stitch before taking it to the back *(diags 3 and 4)*.

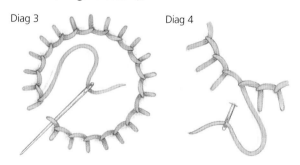

Diag 3   Diag 4

- Alternating between white and orange, stitch a ring of French knots inside the circle and a single white knot at the centre.

- Starting at the centre, work three circles in running stitch, using honey *(diag 5)*.

- Using orange, stitch the outer circle in running stitch.

- Alternating tan and straw, stitch a detached chain for each petal.

Diag 5

Flower two

- Using tan, work blanket stitch around the inner circle, keeping the rays of the stitches towards the centre. Close the circle by working the last stitch under the first stitch, as you did in the first flower.

- Fill the centre with closely worked French knots, using orange.

- Stitch detached chains using straw, around the inner circle *(diag 6)*.

- Using white and honey, stitch the remaining two circles in running stitch.

Diag 6

- Using honey, embroider the petals in detached chain, placing a stitch in each gap between the running stitches.

Flower three

- Using straw, stitch a French knot at the centre of the flower and work another six knots around the centre knot.

flower 2

flower 4

flower 1

flower 3

flower 5

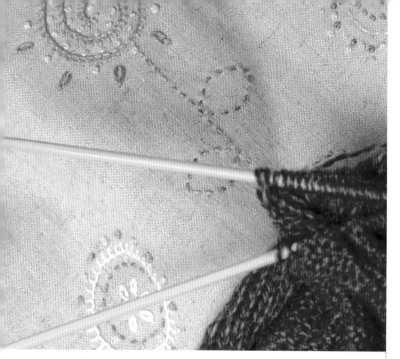

Flower five

- Stitch a French knot at the centre, using tan, and work six detached chains around the knot using orange.
- Using honey, stitch evenly spaced French knots around the flower.
- Work even running stitches around the middle circle, using tan.
- Stitch French knots around the outer circle, alternating orange and straw.
- Using straw, work a French knot on the outside of each orange knot *(diag 9)*.

Diag 9

- Embroider six white detached chains around the French knot centre *(diag 7)*.

Diag 7

- Using orange, work the inner circle in running stitch. Work the outer circle in blanket stitch, using white and keeping the rays of the stitches facing out. Complete the last stitch in the circle as before.
- Stitch detached chains between the two circles, using straw. Begin each stitch just next to the orange circle and finish at the inside edge of the white circle.
- Alternating tan and honey, work French knots around the outer edge of the flower, wrapping the thread twice around the needle for each knot *(diag 8)*.

Flower four

Diag 8

- Starting at the centre of the flower, embroider a spiral in blanket stitch in honey, keeping the rays of the stitches facing out.
- Using tan, stitch French knots along the inside edge of the spiral and at the marked positions around it.
- Stitch the petals in detached chain, using orange.

How to make the bag

See page 108 for instructions.

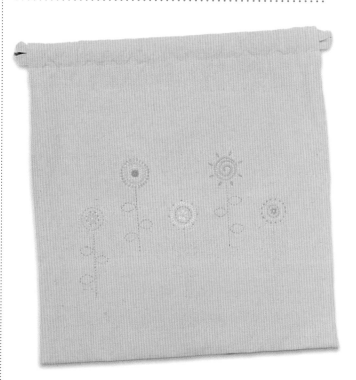

The bag measures 40cm (16") square.

all that glitters

YOU WILL NEED

SUPPLIES
> Scarf

THREADS
> Stranded cotton to match the beads

BEADS
> Bugle beads
> Flat sequins, round or square

EQUIPMENT
> Magic tape
> Tape measure or ruler
> No. 10 between needle

stitches used

attaching sequins with back stitch, page 117

beading with running stitch, page 83

 **SUPER EASY**

Getting started

Preparing the scarf for beading

Place the scarf flat on the table. Measure 8cm (3 ⅛") above the fringe at the sides and at intervals across each end of the scarf. Mark the positions with pins.

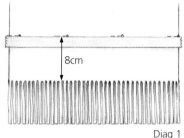

8cm

Diag 1

Place a length of magic tape along the pins to mark the first row of stitching *(diag 1)*.

How to stitch the border

Stitch the bugle beads and sequins in place with one strand of matching thread.

Order of work

- Knot the end of the thread and take two tiny stitches at the edge of the scarf, just above the tape, to secure.
- Stitch a row of bugle beads in place with running stitch along the edge of the tape, spacing the beads evenly *(diag 2)*.

Diag 2

- After every five or six beads, turn the scarf to the wrong side and secure the thread with two tiny stitches behind the last bead *(diag 3)*.

Diag 3

- Remove the tape once the row is complete.
- Measure 2cm (¾") from the row of bugle beads and place a length of tape across the scarf in the same way as before.
- Stitch a row of sequins in place with back stitch, working along the edge of the tape *(diag 4)*.

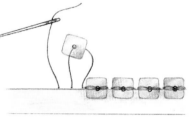

Diag 4

Remember to secure the thread at regular intervals. Remove the tape.

- Stitch another two rows of bugle beads and one row of sequins, spaced 2cm (¾") apart.

YOU WILL NEED

FABRIC

> 25cm (10") square of pink cotton print

SUPPLIES

> 25cm (10") square of lightweight fusible interfacing
> 7 x 2cm (3/4") light pink flower motifs
> Straw bag

THREADS

> Stranded cotton
  Light yellow-green
  Pale yellow
> No. 8 perlé cotton
  Pale pink
> No. 8 variegated perlé cotton
  Fuchsia

BEADS

> 11 x 4mm (3/16") yellow-green round glass beads

BUTTONS

> 4 x 12mm (1/2") shell buttons
> 5 x 12mm (1/2") pearly white flower buttons

EQUIPMENT

> Thimble
> Tracing paper
> Fine black pen
> Fine water-soluble fabric marker
> No. 7 sharp needle
> No. 8 crewel needle

☺☺☺☺ **VERY EASY**

spring time

stitches used

back stitch, page 115

beading, page 115

blanket stitch, page 118

detached chain, page 121

french knot, page 122

technique used

attaching buttons, page 111

Getting started

See the liftout pattern sheet for the embroidery design.

Fuse the piece of interfacing to the wrong side of the pink cotton with a warm iron. Cut the fabric to 22cm (8 5/8") square, cutting along the grain of the fabric (see page 10).

Fold the fabric into quarters and finger press lightly to mark the folds.

Transferring the design

Using the pen, trace the design and placement marks onto the tracing paper. Use the water-soluble fabric marker to transfer the design onto the fabric over a window or light box (see page 18).

How to stitch the design

When you stitch with more than one strand of thread in the needle, remember to strip the threads and keep them untwisted while you stitch (see page 17).

Use the crewel needle when you stitch with two strands of cotton and the sharp needle for all other stitching.

Order of work

Large flowers

- Using the fuchsia variegated perlé cotton, stitch the outline of the four large flowers with rounded petals in back stitch.

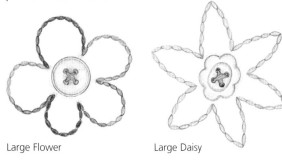

Large Flower   Large Daisy

- Stitch the outline of the five large daisies in back stitch, using pale pink perlé thread.

Leaves

Using two strands of yellow-green, work the centre vein and outline of the leaves in back stitch.

Tiny daisies

- Stitch detached chains for the five petals of each tiny daisy with two strands of pale yellow (see page 121).

- Using two strands of yellow-green, work a French knot with two wraps at the centre of each daisy (diag 1).

Diag 1

- Stitch groups of three French knots at each of the marked positions using the same thread. Secure the thread after each group of knots.

Pink flower motifs

- If your flower motifs are joined as a trim, carefully clip between the flowers to separate them.

- Secure two strands of yellow-green thread on the back at the marked position for a flower motif. Bring the thread to the front and stitch through the centre of one motif (diag 2).

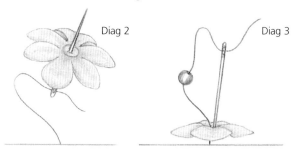

Diag 2   Diag 3

- Take the needle and thread through a green bead and back through the flower and fabric (diag 3).

- Pull the stitch taut and take a second stitch through the flower and bead. Secure and trim the thread on the back. Attach the other six flowers in the same way, securing the thread after each flower.

Button flower centres

Using two strands of pale yellow, attach a shell button at the centre of each large round petal flower and a flower button at the centre of the large pale pink daisies. Attach each button with several cross stitches (see page 111). Secure the thread after each button.

How to attach the embroidered patch to the bag

Preparing the embroidered patch

Rinse the embroidery in cold water to remove any traces of the fabric marker. Leave to dry and press (see pages 19 and 22).

Attaching the patch to the bag

It can be very hard on your fingers when you stitch onto stiff surfaces, so we recommend that you use a thimble when attaching the patch to the bag.

- Fold a 1.5cm ($5/8$") seam allowance to the back along each side. Press and tack in place *(diag 4)*.
- Centre the patch on one side of the straw bag and hold in place with pins pushed into the bag *(diag 5)*. Tack the patch in place and remove the pins.
- Beginning at one corner, work blanket stitch around the edge of the patch using three strands of yellow-green thread in the sharp needle. Work the stitches in a stabbing motion, 6mm ($1/4$") apart (see diags 1 & 2 on page 37).
- Work two stitches into the same hole to turn a corner *(diag 6)*. To finish, stitch a green bead in place at each corner over the blanket stitches.

Diag 4

Diag 5

Diag 6

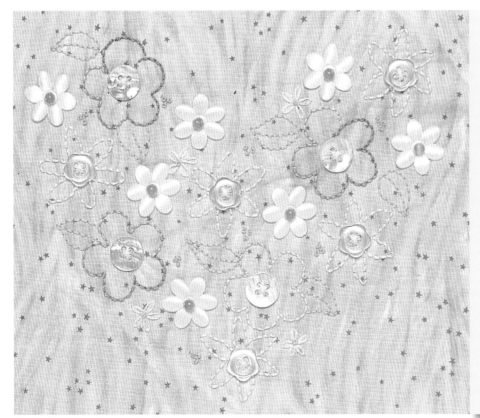

THE BEAUTY OF PATCHES

Embroidered patches like this one or the tiny one on the baby body suit on page 64, can be stitched to many different items such as cushions, book covers, bags and clothing. Patches are really easy to handle while you stitch, because you are only working on a small piece of fabric, unlike larger items, which can be a little tricky at times.

The embroidered patch measures 19cm square (7 $1/2$").

YOU WILL NEED

SUPPLIES
> Pink placemats

THREADS
> Stranded cotton
  Ecru
  Lime green
  Pale blue
  Pale green
  Pale yellow
  Very light violet

EQUIPMENT
> Tracing paper
> Lightweight card
> Fine black permanent pen
> Fine water-soluble fabric marker
> No. 8 crewel needle
> Large yarn darner

stitch used

straight stitch,
page 123

 **SUPER EASY**

starburst

Getting started

See the liftout pattern sheet for the embroidery design and template.

Transferring the design

- Using the black pen, trace dots for the star centres onto the tracing paper.

- Position the tracing parallel to the right hand side of a placemat. Pin the tracing in place.

- Use the large needle to punch a hole in the paper at each marked dot. Mark a dot on the placemat through each hole with the water-soluble fabric marker *(diag 1)*. Remove the tracing.

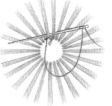

Diag 1

- Make a template for the circles form the card (see page 19). Punch a hole at the centre with a hole-punch.

- Centre the template over a marked dot and trace around the outer circle with the fabric marker *(diag 2)*. Repeat for the other circles.

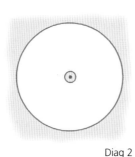

Diag 2

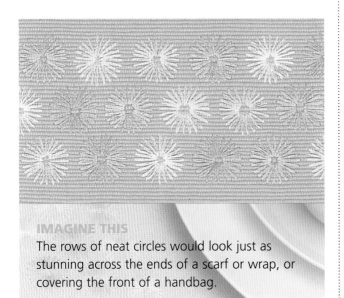

IMAGINE THIS

The rows of neat circles would look just as stunning across the ends of a scarf or wrap, or covering the front of a handbag.

How to stitch the design

All embroidery is stitched with three strands of thread. Strip the threads and keep them untwisted while you work (see page 17).

Order of work

- Tie a knot at the end of the thread. Bring the thread to the front next to the centre dot. Take a straight stitch to the outer edge and emerge just next to the first stitch *(diag 3)*.

Diag 3

- Work a second straight stitch next to the first *(diag 4)*.

Diag 4

- Continue to work straight stitches around the circle in this way, keeping the stitches close together around the centre and evenly spaced on the outer edge.

- To secure the thread, work three or four tiny stitches at the centre of the star into the stitches on the back of the work *(diag 5)*.

Diag 5

- Stitch all the stars in this way, changing colours as you go.

Finishing

Rinse the placemat in cold water to remove any traces of the fabric marker. Leave to dry and press from the wrong side while still damp (see pages 19 and 22).

CAN I WASH THE EMBROIDERED PLACEMATS?

- Most embroidered table linen can be machine washed on a gentle cycle at 40°C (104°F).

- An oxygen based stain remover can be applied before washing if necessary.

- To protect the embroidery while washing, place the linen inside a pillowcase.

- Press while it is still damp on a well padded surface, always with the embroidered side down.

😊😊😊 VERY EASY

tea break

Getting started

See the liftout pattern sheet for the embroidery design.

Transferring the design

Using the fabric marker, transfer the design directly onto the fabric over a window or light box (see page 18).

How to stitch the fuchsia

Flowers

- Using two strands of medium pink thread, begin at the tip of a dark petal and stitch the outline in stem stitch *(diag 1)*. Stitch the outline of the second dark petal and the three lighter middle petals in the same way.

- Use the same thread to stitch the outline of the two remaining petals in back stitch *(diag 2)*.

Diag 1

Diag 2

SUPPLIES

> Cream tray cloth or napkin

THREADS

> Stranded cotton
  Candy pink
  Grass green
  Light pink
  Medium pink
  Yellow-green

EQUIPMENT

> Fine black pen
> Fine water-soluble fabric
  marker
> Tracing paper
> No. 9 crewel needle

stitches used

back stitch, page 115

blanket stitch, page 118

stem stitch, page 123

straight stitch, page 124

Angle the stitches towards the base of the leaf and keep them close together along the centre vein *(diag 5)*. At the top of the vein work all the stitches into the same hole in the fabric and secure the last stitch with a long anchoring stitch to create a tip *(diag 6)*.

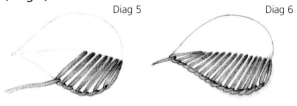

Diag 5   Diag 6

- Beginning at the base of the leaf, stitch the opposite side in a similar way *(diag 7)*. Anchoring the last stitch on the marked line.

Stems

- Begin at the base and stitch the main stem in back stitch with two strands of grass green. End off the thread at the base of the top flower.

Diag 7

- Start a new thread at the tip of the flower and continue in back stitch over the centre vein of the top leaf *(diag 8)*.

- Stitch the stalks of the remaining leaves and the bud in the same way.

Diag 8

Stamens

Use a single strand of the darkest pink for the flower stamens. Work each stitch from just above the flower to the tip of each stamen *(diag 9)*. Work some stitches over the stems.

Diag 9

Finishing

Rinse the embroidery to remove any traces of the water-soluble fabric marker (see page 19).

Gently press the tray cloth on a well padded surface (see page 22).

- Using two strands of light pink, start just inside the outline and fill a middle petal with close rows of stem stitch *(diag 3)*. Fill the remaining two middle petals in the same way.

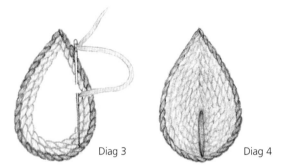

Diag 3   Diag 4

- Use a single strand of candy pink to work a straight stitch over the stitching at the base of each of the light pink petals for the veins *(diag 4)*.

- Using the medium pink thread, fill the two dark petals.

The stamens are stitched after the leaves and stems.

Bud

Use two strands of the darkest pink to stitch the three petals in the same way as the flower petals.

Leaves

The leaves are worked in blanket stitch, using one strand of either grass green or yellow-green.

- Bring the thread to the front at the base of the leaf and work a detached chain without anchoring the loop.

- Continue in blanket stitch along the side of the leaf.

candy heart

YOU WILL NEED

SUPPLIES
> Very light pistachio green T shirt

THREADS
> Stranded cotton Candy pink

BEADS
> Clear candy pink petite beads

EQUIPMENT
> 15cm (6") square of lightweight water-soluble stabiliser eg Solvy
> 15cm (6") square of light-weight fusible interfacing
> 10cm (4") embroidery hoop
> Fine permanent pen
> Sharp lead pencil
> Fine water-soluble fabric marker
> No. 8 and no. 10 sharp needles

stitches used

beading, page 115

french knot, page 122

straight stitch, page 124

HOW DO I KNOW IF A THREAD IS COLOURFAST?

When you are stitching with strong colours on items such as clothing, that need regular washing, it is a good idea to test the colourfastness of your thread before you begin. There is nothing more upsetting than seeing your efforts ruined by colour running into the fabric.

To test, wet the thread thoroughly and place it on a piece of tissue or paper towel. If colour starts seeping into the tissue, the thread is not colourfast and you should avoid using it for stitching on clothing.

 VERY EASY

Getting started

See the liftout pattern sheet for the embroidery design.

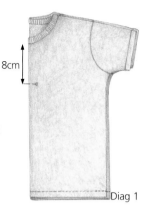

Diag 1

- Turn the T shirt to the wrong side.

  Fold in half and mark the centre front with a pin 8cm (3 1/8") from the neckline *(diag 1)*. Unfold and with the pencil, mark the centre front. Remove the pin.

- Centre the interfacing over the mark and fuse in place on the wrong side, taking care not to stretch the fabric.

- Turn the T shirt to the right side. From the wrong side push a pin through the fabric at the marked centre.

  Mark a dot on the right side and remove the pin.

Transferring the design

- Using the permanent pen, transfer the design onto the water-soluble stabiliser (see page 19).

- Lay the T shirt on a table and temporarily place a book or similar inside, behind the area which is to be embroidered.

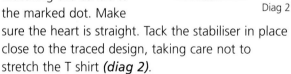

Diag 2

- Position the tracing over the T shirt, matching the centre to the marked dot. Make sure the heart is straight. Tack the stabiliser in place close to the traced design, taking care not to stretch the T shirt *(diag 2)*.

- Use the water-soluble marker to mark dots at 2.5cm (1") intervals around the neckline.

- Place the T shirt front in the hoop, without stretching the knitted fabric (see page 21).

How to stitch the heart

The French knots and crosses are stitched with three strands of thread in the larger needle. When you are stitching with more than one strand, remember to strip the threads and keep them untwisted while you stitch (see page 17).

Use one strand of thread and the small needle for attaching the beads.

Order of work

Heart

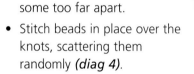

Diag 3

- Working within the design lines, cover the heart with closely worked French knots. It is best to fill the shape as you work to place the knots evenly *(diag 3)*.

  If you scatter the knots over the shape and then fill in the gaps, you can easily have an uneven look, with some knots too crowded and some too far apart.

Diag 4

- Stitch beads in place over the knots, scattering them randomly *(diag 4)*.

Neckline

Work two straight stitches to form a cross over each marked dot around the neckline.

Finishing

Diag 5

- Remove the water-soluble stabiliser (see page 20).

- On the wrong side, peel the interfacing away and trim it carefully, close to the embroidery *(diag 5)*.

LOOSEN UP If you skim the needle between the layers of fabric between each cross, you will avoid long threads showing on the back (see diag 9, page 66). Keep the thread loose between the crosses or you will lose the stretch in the fabric.

butterflies

YOU WILL NEED

SUPPLIES
> Cream self-patterned cushion

THREADS
> Stranded cotton
  Blue-violet
  Candy pink
  China blue
  Light rose pink
  Medium rose pink
  Mocha
  Violet
> Stranded variegated cotton
  Grass green

EQUIPMENT
> Fine water-soluble fabric
  marker or sharp pencil
> Tape measure or ruler
> No. 5 and no. 8
  crewel needles

stitches used

back stitch, page 115

detached chain, page 121

french knot, page 122

stem stitch, page 123

Getting started

See the liftout pattern sheet for the embroidery designs for the butterflies. The flowers of the fabric pattern have been highlighted with stitching.

We have included two flower designs in the liftout pattern, so you can transfer them if you want to stitch on a plain cushion cover or if you can't find a suitable pattern on your cushion.

Remove the insert from the cushion cover.

WHY USE STRANDED THREAD?

Stranded threads are very versatile as you can easily change the appearance and thickness of your stitches. The more strands you work with, the bigger your stitches will be. On this design the lines around the leaves are made a little finer by using only two strands, while the flower petals are worked with three and the plump French knots in the flower centres are worked with six strands.

Tracing and transferring the design

- Trace around selected sections of the pattern in your fabric using a fine water-soluble fabric marker or pencil.
- Transfer the butterflies onto the fabric between the flowers using a window or lightbox (see page 18).

How to stitch the design

Use the no. 5 needle when stitching the French knots and the no. 8 needle for all other stitching.

When you are working with more than one strand of thread, remember to strip the threads and keep them untwisted while you stitch (see page 17).

Order of work

Flowers

- Use three strands of the blue-violet thread to work back stitch around the edges of the flower petals.
- Stitch three large detached chains on each petal, using three strands of the China blue thread. The position of the detached chains should vary a little from petal to petal.
- Use all six strands of violet to work the French knots at the centre of each flower.

Leaves

Work the leaves in back stitch with two strands of variegated green.

Butterflies

- Stitch the body of the butterfly in stem stitch, using three strands of mocha.

  Work French knots for the head and eyes.

  Stitch the antennae with a single strand of the same colour, adding a detached chain at the ends for the smaller butterfly *(diag 1)*.

  Diag 1

- Embroider the lines for the wings with two strands of thread, using the three shades of pink.
- Work the markings on the wings of the large butterfly in detached chain with two strands of China blue. Stitch French knots with two strands of blue-violet for the markings on the wings of the smaller butterfly.

AROUND THE BEND

When you work stem stitch around curves, turn the fabric as you go, so you always stitch with the thread to the outside of the curve, and keep the stitches a little shorter.

 EASY

beaded hearts

Getting started

See the liftout pattern sheet for the embroidery design and bag pattern piece.

Wash and press the cotton twill before you begin (see page 16).

Cutting out

- To make the pattern piece for the front and back, trace the cutting lines and placement marks onto the interfacing and cut out.

- Referring to the cutting layout, mark out the front and back on the cotton twill with the water-soluble marker, aligning each with the straight grain of the fabric (see page 10).

- Where pattern pieces are not provided, cut the pieces according to the measurements below.

Cut two pieces, each 86.5cm x 6cm wide (34 1/2" x 2 3/8") for the side and base gusset

Cut four pieces, each 73cm x 5cm wide (28 3/4" x 2") for the handles

Cutting layout

1. Front and back (bag and lining)
2. Side and base gusset (bag and lining)
3. Handles

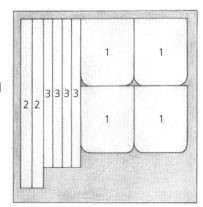

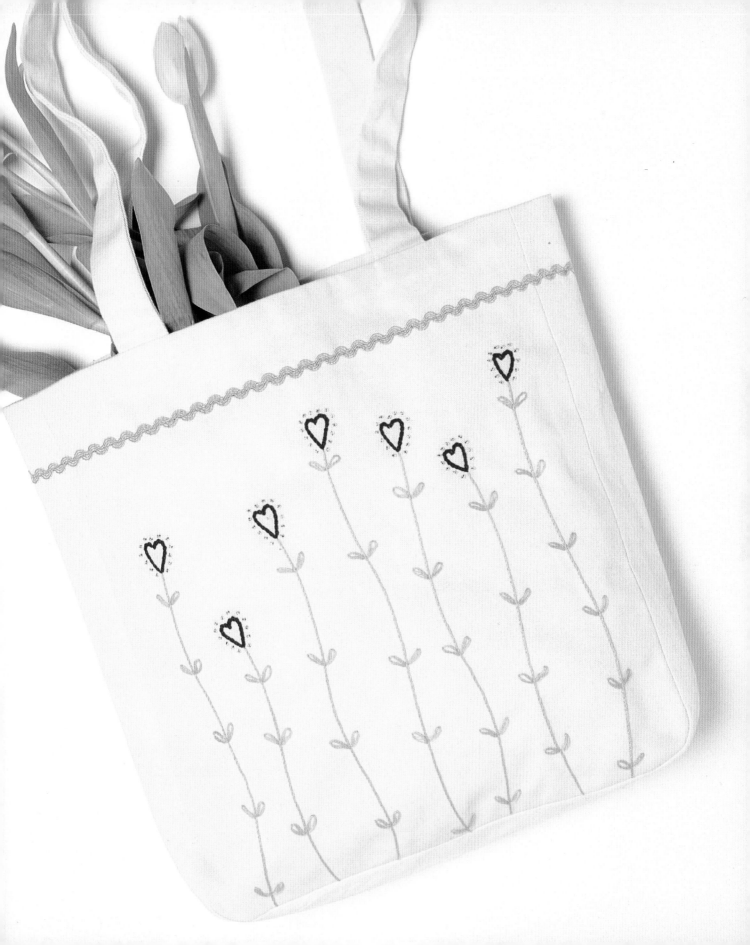

Preparing the bag front for embroidery

Following the manufacturer's instructions, use fabric sealer on the raw edges of one bag piece for the front to prevent the fabric from fraying while you stitch. Leave the piece to dry.

Transferring the design

- Using a pen, trace the design and cutting lines onto the tracing paper.
- Align the marked cutting lines with the edges of the prepared fabric piece and transfer the design over a window or light box, using the fabric marker (see page 18).

How to stitch the heart flowers

Use the no. 7 crewel needle for stranded threads and the no. 10 crewel needle for the beading.

When you are stitching with more than one strand of thread, remember to strip the threads and keep them untwisted while you stitch (see page 17).

Order of work

Hearts

The hearts are stitched in chain stitch, using three strands of cherry red thread.

- Rotate the fabric and begin stitching at the base of the heart. Work small chain stitches along one side of the heart *(diag 1)*.
- Anchor the last stitch at the top of the heart *(diag 2)*.

Diag 1

Diag 2

- Re-emerge inside of the last stitch *(diag 3)*.

Diag 3   Diag 4

- Stitch the second side of the heart in the same way as before and anchor the last stitch at the base *(diag 4)*.

Stems and leaves

The stems and leaves are stitched using three strands of green. If necessary, join new threads by following the hint on page 104.

- Rotate the fabric to work the stems.

  Beginning with a short stitch at the base of each heart, work the stems in stem stitch *(diag 5)*.

Diag 5   Diag 6

- Work each stem almost to the lower edge of the fabric *(diag 6)*.
- Embroider each leaf with a large detached chain. Take care not to pull the stitches taut as this will make them very thin.

The bag front measures 30cm x 27cm wide (12" x 10 5/8").

Beading

The beads are attached with a single strand of cherry red thread. Turn the work over after every five or six beads and secure the thread on the back (see diag 3, page 83).

- Bring the thread to the front at the marked position for the first bead.

- Thread a bead onto the needle and take the needle to the back, a short distance from where it emerged, to fit the width of the bead *(diag 7)*.

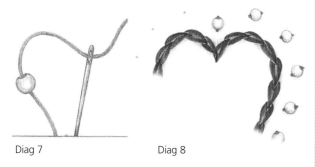

Diag 7   Diag 8

- Attach the remaining beads around the heart in this way, varying the direction of the stitch for each bead *(diag 8)*.

- Rinse the bag front in cold water to remove any traces of the fabric marker (see page 19).

How to make the bag

See page 109 for instructions.

JOINING A NEW THREAD IN STEM STITCH

You can achieve an invisible join in your stem stitch by following these few easy steps.

- Leaving the last stitch very loose, take the thread to the front of your work a short distance away from the area being stitched. Unthread the needle leaving the thread tail hanging *(fig 1)*.

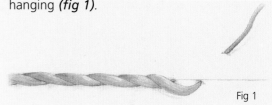

Fig 1

- Secure the new thread on the back and bring it to the front, half way along the last stitch *(fig 2)*.

Fig 2

- Gently pull the old thread tail, pulling the last stitch taut. Turn the work over and pull the old thread to the back and secure.

- Continue working the row of stem stitch with the new thread.

putting it together

Once your stitching is finished you will need to put the pieces together. This is not at all difficult. Just remember to take your time. The instructions and diagrams on the following pages will guide you every step of the way.

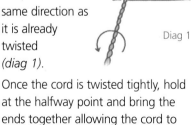

safe sailing

For colour photos and full details, see pages 45 - 47.

All seam allowances are 1cm (3/8"). The shaded areas on the following diagrams indicate the right side of the fabric.

1. Making the cord handle

Cut a 1.6m (2yd 27") length of red and white cord and knot the ends. Place one end under the presser foot of your sewing machine. Keeping the cord taut, twist it in the same direction as it is already twisted (diag 1).

Diag 1

Once the cord is twisted tightly, hold at the halfway point and bring the ends together allowing the cord to twist on itself. Tie the ends together (diag 2).

Diag 2

Using a red thread, wrap the end of the cord firmly just above the knot. Stitch through the wrapping several times to secure (diag 3). Trim the knot and set the cord aside.

wrap   Diag 3

2. Making the bag

From the upper edge, measure 10cm (4") along each side and mark with a pin. Place the handle, with the ends matching the raw edges of the fabric, at the marked positions. Tack the ends securely in place through all layers (diag 4).

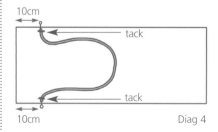

10cm
tack
tack
10cm   Diag 4

Fold the linen in half across the width, with right sides together and matching raw edges, sandwiching the handle between the layers. Pin and stitch the side seams (diag 5).

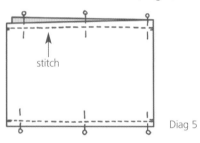

stitch

Diag 5

Press the seams and turn the bag through to the right side.

Cut a 7cm (2 3/4") length of single cord for the button loop. Matching raw edges, place the cord ends over the seam allowance on the right side of the bag at the centre of the upper back edge. Tack in place inside the seam allowance (diag 6).

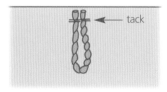

tack

Diag 6

3. Making the lining

Fold the lining piece in half across the width, with right sides together and matching raw edges. Pin and stitch the side seams, leaving a 15cm (6") opening along one side (diag 7).

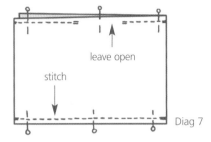

leave open

stitch

Diag 7

Press the seams, including those along the opening. Do not turn to the right side yet.

4. Attaching the lining to the bag

Place the bag inside the lining with right sides together, matching upper raw edges and side seams. The button loop is sandwiched between the layers. Pin and stitch around the upper edge, making sure you don't catch the handle in the seam (diag 8).

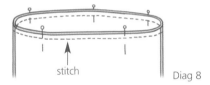

stitch

Diag 8

Turn the bag to the right side through the opening in the lining. Handstitch the opening closed (diag 9).

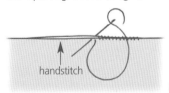

handstitch

Diag 9

Push the lining into the bag and press the upper edge. Top stitch around the upper edge, aligning the edge of your presser-foot with the folded edge of the fabrics (diag 10).

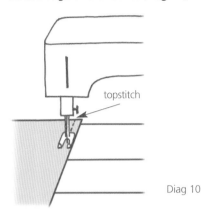

topstitch

Diag 10

5. Finishing

Lay the bag flat and, at the handles, fold the upper edges to the front. With a pin, mark the position for the buttons inside the loop (diag 11).

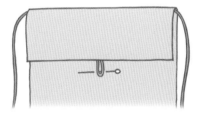

Diag 11

Place the red button over the white button and stitch the pair securely in place at the marked position following the instructions on page 111.

let it snow

For colour photos and full details, see pages 56-59.

Changing the size of the album cover

1. Measure the album from front edge to front edge around the spine using a tape measure (diag 1).

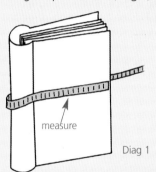

measure

Diag 1

Double this measurement and add 31cm (12 ¼") for the inside flaps and seam allowance. This gives you the width of fabric needed.

2. Measure the height of the album and add 3cm (1 ¼") to the measurement for the seam allowance. This gives you the length of fabric you will need.

All seam allowances are 1.5cm (⅝"). The shaded areas on the following diagrams indicate the right side of the fabric.

1. Making the cover

Fold the furnishing fabric in half across the width with right sides together and matching raw edges.

Pin and stitch across the short end, leaving a 25cm (10") opening (diag 2).

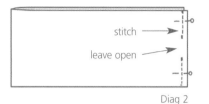

Diag 2

2. Making the flaps

Measure 14cm (5 1/2") in from the foldline on one edge and mark with a pin.

Measure 14cm (5 1/2") in from the stitchline at the opposite end and mark with a pin. Repeat for the remaining long edge.

Pin and stitch the layers together along each side between the pins (diag 3).

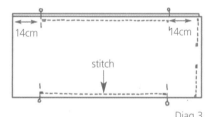

Diag 3

On the upper edge, mark the fold with a pin. Open out the end and bring the pin back to the stitching (diag 4).

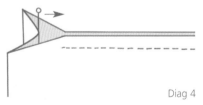

Diag 4

Bring the two new folds evenly together and pin. Complete the stitching through all layers (diag 5).

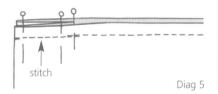

Diag 5

Repeat for the upper edge at the opposite end, matching the seamline to the stitched point (diags 6 & 7).

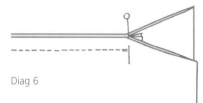

Diag 6

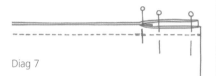

Diag 7

Repeat at each end of the lower edge in the same way.

3. Finishing

Turn the cover to the right side through the opening and carefully push out the corners. Make sure the flaps face towards the inside.

Handstitch the opening closed (diag 8).

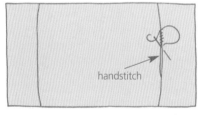

Diag 8

Tuck the the front and back covers of the album into the flaps.

marigolds

For colour photos and full details, see pages 76-81.

All seam allowances are 1cm (3/8") The shaded areas on the following diagrams indicate the right side of the fabric.

1. Preparing the embroidered fabric

Rinse the fabric to remove any traces of the fabric marker (see page 19). Leave to dry.

Place the fabric with the embroidery facing down on a well padded surface and press.

2. Making the bag

With right sides facing and matching raw edges, fold the fabric in half across the width. Measure 6cm (2 3/8") from the top edge and mark with a pin at each side (diag 1).

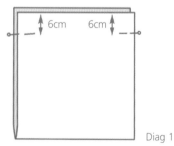

Diag 1

Pin and stitch the side seams from the marked positions to the folded lower edge (diag 2).

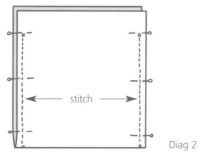

Diag 2

Press the side seams open and turn the bag to the right side.

3. Making the lining

Make the lining in a similar manner to the bag, leaving a 15cm (6") wide opening along one side (diag 3).

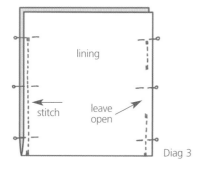

Diag 3

4. Attaching the lining to the bag

Place the bag inside the lining with right sides together and matching raw edges. Pin and stitch along each upper edge (diag 4).

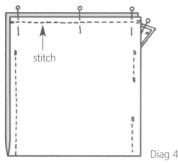

Diag 4

Press the seams open, including those along the opening.

Turn the lining to the right side through the opening. Handstitch the opening closed (diag 5).

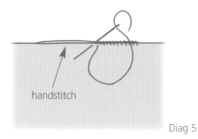

handstitch

Diag 5

At each side of the bag, top stitch 5mm (3/16") from the folded edge around the drawstring opening (diag 6).

Diag 6

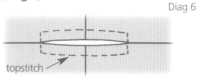

topstitch

Push the lining into the bag and press the upper edge.

5. Making the drawstring channel

Measure 3cm (1 1/4") from the upper edge. Using the fabric marker, rule a line parallel to the edge on each side of the bag. Pin and stitch the layers together along the marked lines to form channels (diag 7).

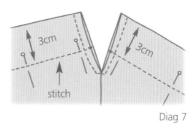

3cm   3cm

stitch

Diag 7

6. Making and inserting the drawstrings

With right sides together and matching raw edges, fold a draw-string piece in half along the length. Pin and stitch, leaving the ends open (diag 8).

Diag 8

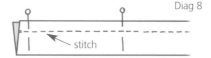

stitch

Turn the piece to the right side through the opening, using a loop-turner or safety pin, and press.

Insert the drawstring through the channels all the way around the bag. Fold the seam allowance at one end to the inside (diag 9).

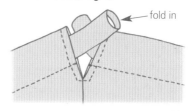

fold in

Diag 9

Insert the raw end into the folded end and top stitch through all layers (diag 10).

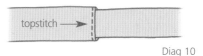

topstitch

Diag 10

Repeat for the second drawstring, inserting it in the opposite direction.

beaded hearts

For colour photos and full details, see pages 100 - 104.

All seam allowances are 1cm (3/8") unless otherwise specified. The shaded areas on the following diagrams indicate the right side of the fabric.

1. Preparing the embroidered piece

Rinse the embroidered front to remove all traces of the fabric marker (see page 19). Leave to dry. Place the embroidery with the right side facing down on a thick towel and press.

2. Making the handles

Place two handle pieces with right sides together, matching raw edges, and pin. Stitch along each long side, leaving the ends open (*diag 1*).

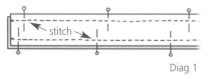

Diag 1

Using a loop turner or safety pin, turn the handle to the right side through one end and press.

Repeat for the second handle.

3. Preparing the side and base gusset

Fold the piece for the bag back in half down the length and mark the fold with a pin at the lower edge. Unfold (*diag 2*). Repeat for the front piece.

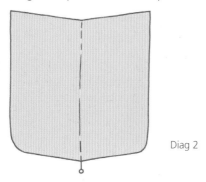

Diag 2

Fold the gusset piece in half across the width and mark with a pin at each side of the fold. Unfold (*diag 3*).

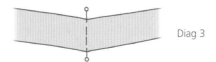

Diag 3

4. Making the bag

With right sides together and matching raw edges, position the gusset over the bag back piece, matching the pins (*diag 4*).

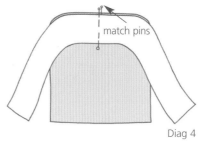

match pins

Diag 4

Pin in place along the base and along each side, easing the gusset piece to fit the corners. Stitch in place (*diag 5*).

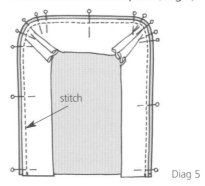

stitch

Diag 5

Attach the front of the bag to the gusset in the same way.

Press the seams open and turn to the right side.

5. Making the lining

Make the lining in a similar way to the bag, leaving a 15cm (6") opening along one side (*diag 6*).

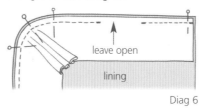

leave open

lining

Diag 6

Do not turn to the right side yet.

6. Attaching the handles

With right sides together and matching raw edges, position the ends of one handle on the back of the bag at the marked positions, making sure the handle is not twisted. Pin and stitch in place (*diag 7*).

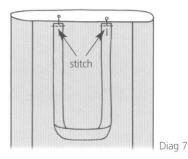

stitch

Diag 7

Repeat for the second handle on the front of the bag.

7. Attaching the lining

With right sides together and matching upper edges and seams, slide the lining over the bag, sandwiching the handles between. Pin and stitch around the upper edge (*diag 8*).

stitch

Diag 8

Turn the bag and lining to the right side through the opening in the lining. Handstitch the opening closed (*diag 9*).

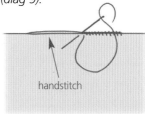

handstitch

Diag 9

Push the lining into the bag and press the upper edge.

8. Attaching the ric rac braid

Measure 4cm (1 1/2") from the upper edge and, using a pencil, rule a line parallel to the upper edge around the bag (diag 10).

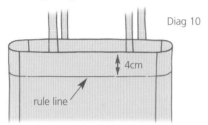

Diag 10

4cm

rule line

Fold under one end of the ric rac braid. Place the ric rac over the ruled line, aligning the folded edge with a back seam (diag 11).

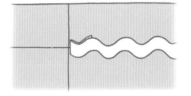

Diag 11

Pin the braid in place over the marked line around the bag. Trim the opposite end of the braid and fold under, butting the fold up against the beginning of the braid. Using matching machine sewing thread, stitch in place along the centre of the braid (diag 12).

Diag 12

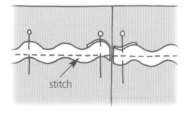

stitch

finishing touches

attaching buttons

Whether you are using buttons as decoration or as a fastener, it is important that they are stitched in place securely. You can use a matching thread if you don't want it to show or a contrasting thread for decorative purposes.

1. Knot the end of a doubled thread. Secure the thread on the wrong side at the position for the button.

2. Bring the thread to the front and through one hole in the button. Centre the button over the stitch (diag 1).

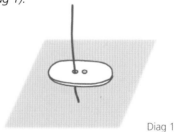

Diag 1

3. Take the needle down through the second hole and through the fabric close to where the thread emerged (diag 2).

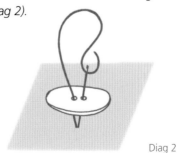

Diag 2

4. Work another 3 – 4 stitches into the pair of holes, taking the needle through the same holes in the fabric (diag 3).

Diag 3

5. End off securely on the back by taking the needle through the stitches on the back several times (diag 4).

Diag 4

6. Buttons with four holes can be stitched in place with two parallel stitches or with a cross stitch.

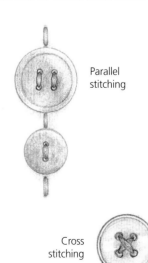

Parallel stitching

Cross stitching

twisted cord

This is a very easy way to make a cord to match your project. You can use a single thread or a bundle of threads to achieve the thickness of the cord you want.

1. Fold the thread(s) in half and knot the ends together.

2. Hold the knotted end securely in place, eg place it under the presser foot of your sewing machine, pin it to a firm surface or ask someone to hold it for you *(diag 1)*.

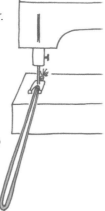

3. Place a pencil through the looped end of the threads.

4. Hold the threads between your thumb and index finger just in front of the pencil to keep it in place *(diag 2)*.

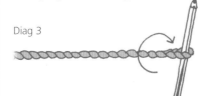

Diag 2

5. Rotate the pencil in a clockwise direction until the threads are tightly twisted *(diag 3)*.

Diag 3

6. Fold the twisted threads in half, making sure the threads are kept taut *(diag 4)*.

Diag 4

7. Keeping the twisted threads fully stretched, release slowly from the folded end until all the cord is twisted onto itself *(diag 5)*.

Diag 5

8. Release the knotted end. Knot the ends together and trim the tails *(diag 6)*.

Diag 6

stitch library

Some of the most used and easiest embroidery stitches are described on the following pages, including ways to stitch on beads and sequins. Take your time, perhaps practise on a small piece of fabric. With each stitch your stitching will improve.

Stitching for left-handers

If you are left handed you will need to work most stitches in the opposite direction to the one described. The stitches are worked as a mirror image to the way right handers work them. To make it easier to follow the instructions you can turn the illustrations upside down or you can place a mirror above the picture and follow the image in the mirror.

Stitches that are worked horizontally are worked in the same way as described in the instructions.

appliqué

Appliqué is a fun and easy way to attach a design to a base fabric. Appliqué paper makes it possible to achieve a quick result. The edges of the fabric are often trimmed with blanket stitch (see page 118). The templates for fused appliqué are mirrored so that the finished design will face in the right direction. It is a good idea to protect your iron and ironing board with a cloth.

1. Trace a template onto the smooth side of the appliqué paper.

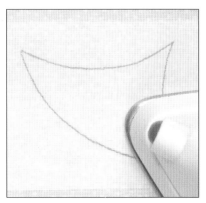

2. Place the appliqué paper, with the smooth side facing up, over the wrong side of the fabric piece. Fuse in place with warm, dry iron.

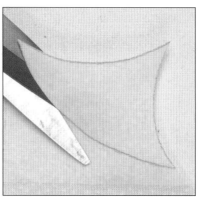

3. Cut out the shape along the traced lines.

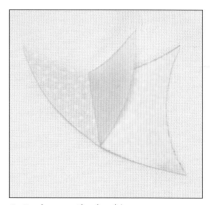

4. Peel away the backing paper.

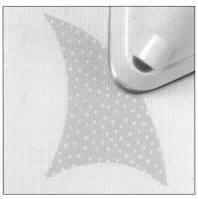

5. Position the appliqué piece onto the main fabric, with the right side of the fabric facing up. Fuse the piece in place with a warm, dry iron.

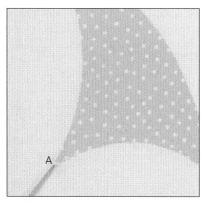

6. Blanket stitch edge. Secure the thread on the back with a knot. Bring the thread to the front at A, just outside the edge of the appliqué piece.

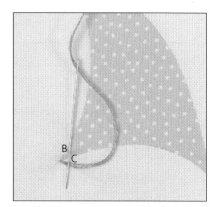

7. Take the needle to the back at B, through the appliqué piece. Emerge at C, just outside the edge. Keep the thread under the tip of the needle.

8. Continue in this way along the edge of the appliqué piece, keeping the stitches even.

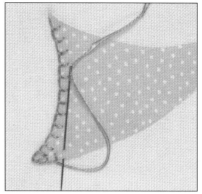

9. Turning a corner. Work three blanket stitches into the same hole to turn a corner or point. Rotate the fabric.

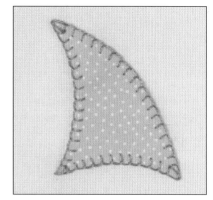

10. Continue stitching in this way to outline the shape.

back stitch

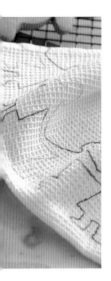

Back stitch is a line stitch and is well suited to following tight curves. Work the stitches from right to left.

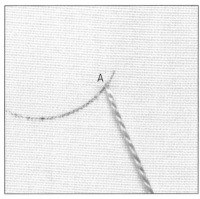

1. Bring the thread to the front at A, a stitch length from the right hand end of the marked line.

2. Take the needle to the back at B at the beginning of the marked line. Emerge at C. The distance from A to C should be the same as the distance from A to B.

3. Pull the thread through to complete the first stitch. Take the needle to the back at A, through the same hole in the fabric. Emerge at D. The distance from C to D is the same as from A to C.

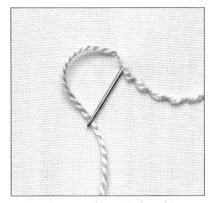

4. Continue working stitches this way, keeping them even. To finish, take the needle to the back and end off.

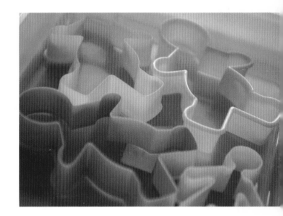

beading – attaching a single bead

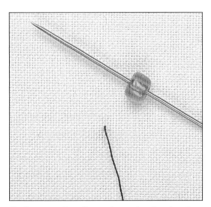

1. Secure the thread on the back of the fabric and bring it to the front. Thread the bead onto the needle.

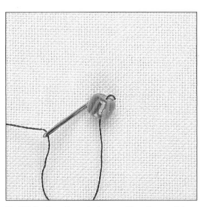

2. Slide the bead down the thread to the fabric. Take the needle to the back at the end of the bead.

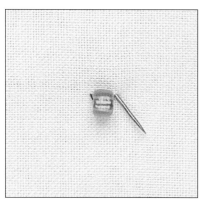

3. Pull the thread through. Re-emerge at the other end of the bead.

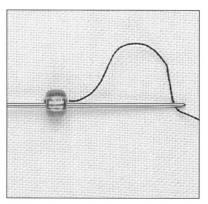

4. Take the needle through the bead again.

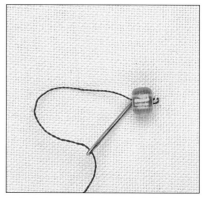

5. Pull the thread through. Take the needle to the back of the fabric at the end of the bead.

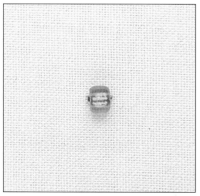

6. Pull the thread through. End off on the back of the fabric.

beading – rows of beads (back stitch)

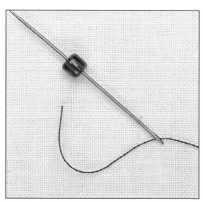

1. Secure the thread on the back of the fabric and bring it to the front. Thread a bead onto the needle.

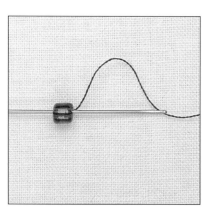

2. Attach the bead following steps 2 - 4 for attaching a single bead on pages 115 and 116.

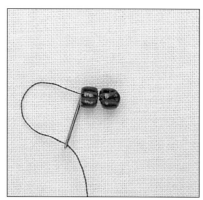

3. Pull the thread through. Thread a second bead onto the needle. Take the needle to the back of the fabric at the end of the second bead.

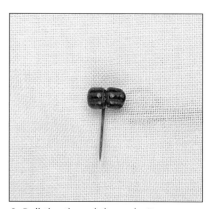

4. Pull the thread through. Re-emerge between the two beads.

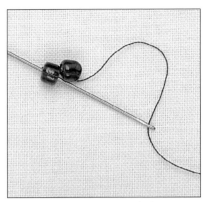

5. Take the needle through the second bead again.

6. Pull the thread through. Thread a third bead onto the needle.

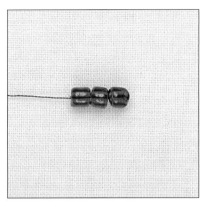

7. Secure the third bead to the fabric in the same way.

8. Continue attaching the row of beads in this way. After the last bead, take the thread to the back of the fabric and secure.

beading - row of sequins (back stitch)

1. Secure the thread on the back of the fabric. Bring it to the front through the hole in the sequin.

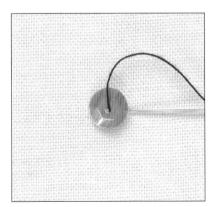

2. Take the needle to the back alongside the right hand edge of the sequin.

3. Pull the thread through. Emerge alongside the left hand edge.

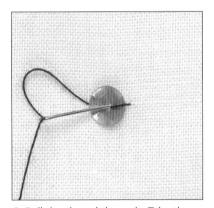

4. Pull the thread through. Take the needle to the back through the centre hole.

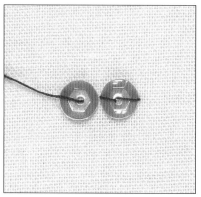

5. Pull the thread through. Position a second sequin to the left of the first sequin. Bring the thread to the front through the hole.

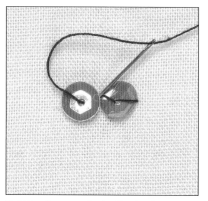

6. Take the needle to the back alongside the right hand edge.

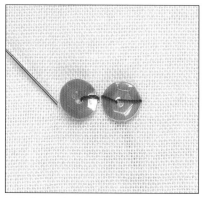

7. Pull the thread through. Re-emerge alongside the left hand edge.

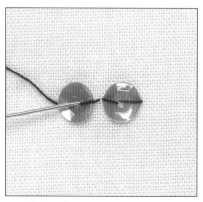

8. Pull the thread through. Take the needle to the back through the centre hole.

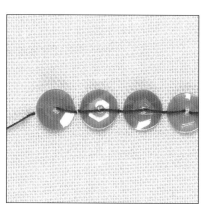

9. Pull the thread through. Continue attaching sequins in the same manner.

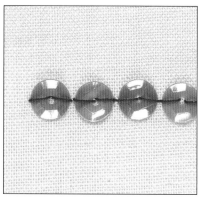

10. After attaching the last sequin, end off the thread on the back of the fabric.

blanket stitch

Traditionally used for edging blankets and rugs, blanket stitch can be worked as a surface embroidery stitch as well as an edging stitch and is commonly used for appliqué (see page 113). Work the stitches from left to right, keeping the thread below the needle.

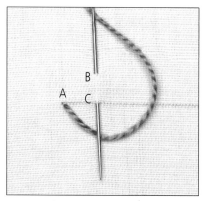

1. Bring the thread to the front at A. Take the needle from B to C. Make sure the thread is under the tip of the needle.

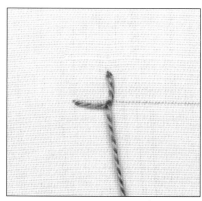

2. Pull the thread towards you until the loop rests gently against the emerging thread.

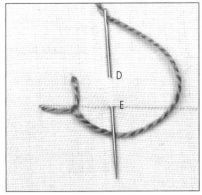

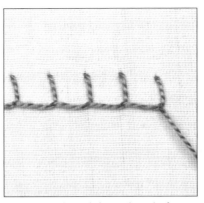

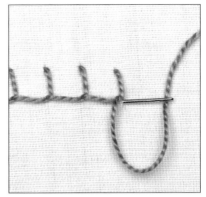

3. Take the needle from D to E, a short distance from the previous stitch. Make sure the thread is under the tip of the needle.

4. Pull the thread through as before. Continue working stitches in this way.

5. To finish, take the needle to the back of the fabric just over the last loop and secure.

blanket stitch pinwheel

Often called blanket pinwheels, these are formed from blanket stitches worked in a circle radiating from the centre.

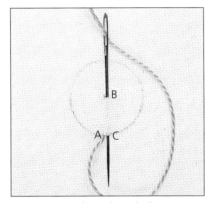

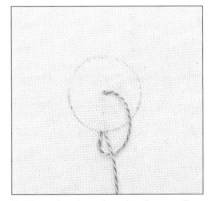

1. Draw a circle and mark the centre. Bring the thread to front at A. Take the needle from the centre B to C.

2. Place the thread under the needle tip. Begin to pull the thread through, pulling away from the circle.

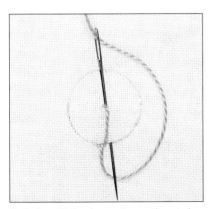

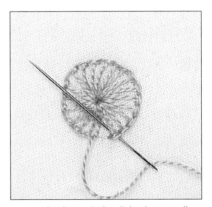

3. Pull until the loop sits on the circle. Take the needle from the centre to the edge. Ensure the thread is under the needle.

4. Continue working stitches around the circle, rotating the fabric as you work.

5. For the last stitch, slide the needle under the first stitch without catching the fabric.

6. Pull the thread through. Take the needle through the centre to complete the pinwheel.

chain stitch

This very versatile stitch can be used as an outline or in close rows as a filling stitch. Take care not to pull the loops too tight as they will lose their rounded shape. The stitch is worked from the top towards you.

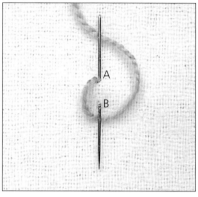

1. Bring the thread to the front at A. Take the needle from A to B, using the same hole in the fabric at A. Loop the thread under the tip of the needle.

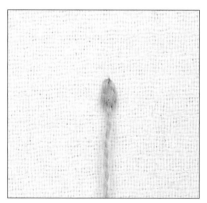

2. Pull the thread through until the loop lies snugly around the emerging thread.

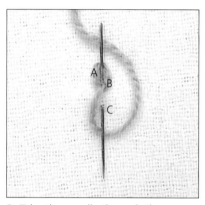

3. Take the needle through the same hole in the fabric at B and emerge at C. Ensure the thread is under the tip of the needle.

4. Pull the thread through as before. Continue working stitches in the same manner for the required distance.

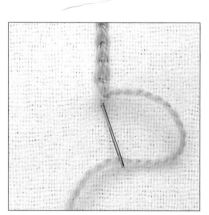

5. To finish, work the last stitch and take the needle to the back of the fabric just over the loop.

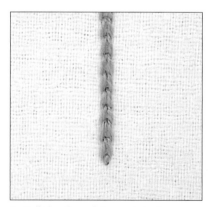

6. Pull the thread through to form a short straight stitch. End off the thread on the back of the fabric.

detached chain

This is also commonly known as lazy daisy. Detached chain is a looped stitch, which can be worked alone or in groups and is often used to create leaves and flowers with each petal being a single detached chain.

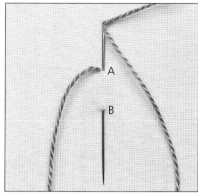

1. Bring the needle to the front at the base of the stitch at A. Take the needle to the back as close as possible to A and emerge at B.

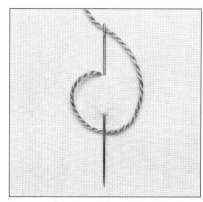

2. Loop the thread in and under the tip of the needle.

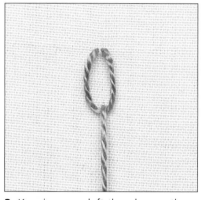

3. Keeping your left thumb over the loop, pull the thread through. The tighter you pull, the thinner the stitch will become.

4. To anchor the stitch, take the thread to the back just over the loop.

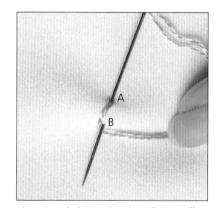

Five petal daisy 1. Bring the needle to the front at A (centre). Take it to the back at A and emerge at B. Loop the thread under needle tip.

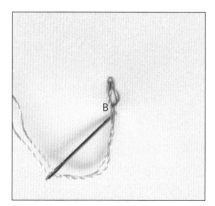

2. Pull the thread through gently. Anchor the stitch by taking the needle to the back over the loop.

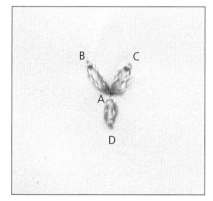

3. Pull the thread through and bring the needle up at A. Work two detached chains from A - C and A - D. Rotate the fabric for each stitch.

4. Work the fourth and fifth detached chains in the spaces between the previous petals to complete the flower.

french knot

The traditional French knot was worked with one wrap around the needle, however today it is often worked with more. To create a larger knot, it is neater to use a thicker thread rather than making too many wraps.

1. Bring the thread to the front. Hold the thread firmly with your thumb and index finger 3cm (1¼") away from the fabric.

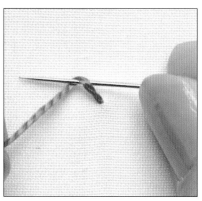

2. Bring the thread over the needle. Ensure the needle points away from the fabric.

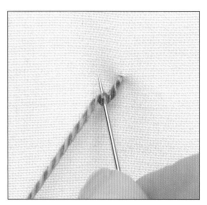

3. Wrap the thread around the needle. Keeping the thread taut, begin to turn the point of the needle towards the fabric.

4. Take the needle to the back 1 - 2 fabric threads away from the emerging thread.

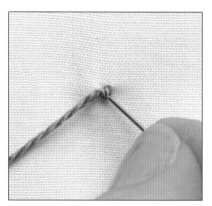

5. Slide the knot down the needle onto the fabric. Pull the thread until the knot sits firmly around the needle.

6. Hold the wraps in place with your thumb. Push the needle through the wraps. Pull from the back until a firm knot forms on the fabric.

running stitch

This is one of the quickest and easiest stitches of all but it will not cover a marked line. Make the stitches uniform in length and slightly longer on the front than on the back. Running stitch is worked from right to left.

1. Bring the thread to the front on the right hand end of the line to be stitched.

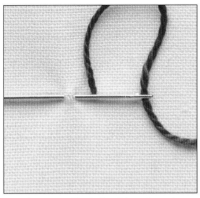

2. Take a small stitch, skimming the needle beneath the fabric along the line.

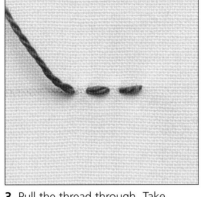

3. Pull the thread through. Take another stitch as before, ensuring the stitch is the same length as the previous stitch.

4. Continue in the same manner to the end of the line.

stem stitch

This very versatile stitch is ideal for fine lines and curves. It can also be used as a filling stitch when worked in close rows, like the petals on 'tea break' on page 90. Work stem stitch from left to right, keeping the thread below the needle.

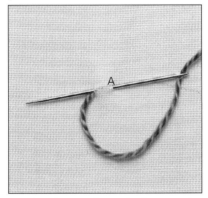

1. Bring the needle to the front at the left hand end of the line. With the thread below the needle, take it to the back at A. Re-emerge at the end of the line.

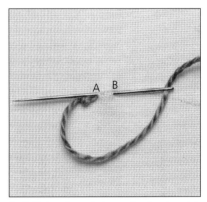

2. Pull the thread through. Again with the thread below the needle, take the needle from B to A.

3. Pull the thread through. Continue working the stitches in the same way, always keeping the thread below the needle and the stitches the same size.

4. To end off, take the needle to the back for the last stitch but do not re-emerge. Secure the thread on the back.

straight stitch

This is the most basic embroidery stitch of all. It can be worked in any direction and to any length.

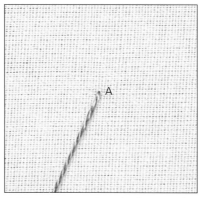

1. Bring the thread to the front at the beginning of the stitch, A.

2. Take the needle to the back at the end of the stitch, B.

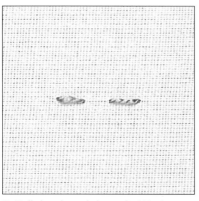

3. Pull the thread through. Work a second stitch in the same manner.

4. Straight stitches worked at different angles.

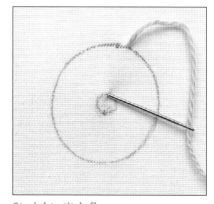

Straight stitch flower
1. Bring the thread to the front on the outer circle. Take it to the back on the inner circle.

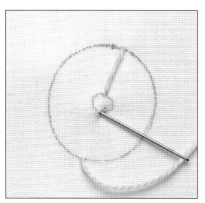

2. Pull the thread through. Emerge on the opposite side of the outer circle. Take the needle to the back on the inner circle.

3. Continue working stitches, varying their length slightly and always working the stitches roughly opposite each other.

Special thanks

Without the contribution of the following designers and stitchers,
Stitching for beginners and beyond
would not have been possible.

sunshine, circles and stripes, kitty kat, curious cats, butterflies
designed and stitched by **ANNA SCOTT**

buttoned up
designed by **MELINDA BARTA**, stitched by **JANET REDMAN**

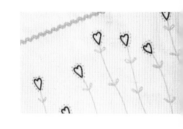

paper dolls
designed by **ANNA SCOTT**, stitched by **MARIAN CARPENTER**

happiness, tall ships, safe sailing
designed by **ANNA SCOTT**, stitched by **TESSA CHAPLIN**

billy buttons
designed and stitched by **ANNICK LEFEBVRE**

daisy chain, starburst, tea break
designed by **ANNA SCOTT**, stitched by **KRIS RICHARDS**

pebbles, all that glitters, spring time
designed by **ANNA SCOTT**, stitched by **JANET REDMAN**

let it snow, autumn leaves, marigold
designed by **ANNA SCOTT**, stitched by **CECILY DAVEY**

twilight
designed and stitched by **KATE LITTLE**

candy heart
designed and stitched by **LIBBY VATER**

beaded hearts
designed and stitched by **YVETTE STANTON**

Thank you also to **AL-RU FARM, DR AND MRS AKKERMAN** and **ELIZABETH PETERSON**

index